UNBROKEN
A Mother-Daughter Journey of Resilience, Faith and Courage

EGLI COLÓN STEPHENS
EPIGRAPH BY NATALIA HARRIS

©Unbroken

Copyright © 2019 Egli Colón Stephens

ISBN-13: 978-1727107289
ISBN-10: 1727107284

The colored version of all the pictures included in the book are available for view and download on Egli Colón Stephens' website: eglicolonstephens.com

All rights reserved.

No part of this book may be reproduced, stored in a retrieval system, or transmitted by any means, including recording, photocopying, or other electronic methods, without the written permission of the author, except in the case of brief quotations embodied in critical reviews.

Medical Disclaimer: This book which references some medical terms is not intended as a substitute for consultation with a licensed healthcare practitioner, such as your physician.

All Bible quotations are in the New International Version translation, except if stated otherwise.

Cover design by Morenike Olusanya
Cover photographs by Jacqueline Ayala

*This book is for anyone in need of hope.
It is dedicated to my brave and resilient daughter,
Natalia as a reminder of her inner strength and battles won.
Your life is a testament of faith.*

Vivistes para contarlo.

My little one, in giving birth to you, I gave birth to the warrior in me.

Egli Colón Stephens, Ed.D.

You have searched me, Lord and you know me.
-Psalm 139:1

CONTENT

- 18   **CHAPTER 1**   BIRTH OF AN UNWAVERING FAITH
- 27   **CHAPTER 2**   A CHRISTMAS EVE MIRACLE
- 37   **CHAPTER 3**   CHILDREN DO NOT LISTEN TO WHAT WE SAY, THEY WATCH WHAT WE DO
- 43   **CHAPTER 4**   WHATEVER WE SURRENDER TO THE DIVINE WILL BE TRANSFORMED
- 54   **CHAPTER 5**   LIFE AS WE KNEW IT
- 68   **CHAPTER 6**   PRAYING MY WAY THROUGH THIS
- 85   **CHAPTER 7**   READY FOR COMBAT
- 103   **CHAPTER 8**   SUNSHINE ON THE BATTLEFIELD
- 141   **CHAPTER 9**   PERFECTION IN THE IMPERFECTION
- 166   **CHAPTER 10**   I PRAYED TO MY GOD FOR HELP
- 194   **CHAPTER 11**   LET YOUR SPIRIT DANCE
- 223   **CHAPTER 12**   FAITH AND COURAGE IN THE FACE OF ADVERSITY

CONTENT

255 **CHAPTER 13**
LIKE THE PHOENIX, WE RISE

276 **CHAPTER 14**
REDEFINING OUR NEW NORMAL

299 **CHAPTER 15**
PICKING UP THE BROKEN PIECES

317 **CHAPTER 16**
FAITH AND FEAR DO NOT COEXIST
EPIGRAPH BY NATALIA HARRIS

331 **ACKNOWLEDGEMENTS**

FOREWORD

> *There is no greater agony than bearing an untold story inside you.*
>
> - Maya Angelou

The first time I met Dr. Egli Colón Stephens, it was in my first semester at Bronx Community College. I remember that day vividly. Extremely anxious about the college life and coming into a new country, I sat still at the front of the class, my feverish legs caressed by a pair of blue jeans were glued together and my arms folded to my chest. The classroom, filled with unfamiliar faces and equally anxious students was very quiet, unknown to all that the professor, Dr. Egli, was sitting in our midst. She was conducting a brief experiment on student interaction at first sight. When she came up to introduce herself as the professor after about five minutes, everyone smiled and that eased the tension.

The narrative in Unbroken is very symbolic of my first day in Dr. Egli's class. It is of a woman stepping out, in familiar shoes, and using her experiences to ease the tension of many troubled hearts. In this book, you will read about divine love and triumph when Dr. Egli's only daughter, Natalia, faced a near death experience.

Through Unbroken, I was brought back to a book I read in 2017, titled On Truth by Harry G. Frankfurt. My favorite line of the text says,

"Love is nothing but joy with the accompanying idea of an external cause."

With Unbroken, my definition of love and joy transformed. I gained an understanding of how one can choose to love another person fiercely as God loved them rather than loving their neighbor as they loved themselves when they knew, truthfully that they weren't self-sufficient.

You will also learn about total submission in faith. You will see a mother unashamed of being on her knees in God's presence when her feet were not strong enough to climb her mountains. You will see a mother become one with her daughter; the only fruit of her womb, in pain and happiness. You will also see Natalia with love, using her strength and humor to pull her mother through tough days.

In Unbroken, you will learn how to be brave through the eyes of Natalia, a 12-year-old who refused to let her diagnosis weigh her down. She spoke her miracle to life and called the leg diagnosed with cancer "Will," that it "will walk again." Through Natalia, you will understand the fragility of life and how it is accompanied by a type of joy which is only visible to a grateful heart. During chemotherapy, simple actions that Natalia took, such as eating or staying awake became an epitome of favor and beauty, especially for those who prayed relentlessly to keep her alive.

Such moments in Unbroken furthermore exemplified Frankfurt words about how love and joy are different. He wrote, "Love is of external things, and joy is an internal feeling about the external things that we love." And joy is "what follows that passion by which the (individual) passes to greater perfection."

Only love can make one find joy in difficult times and imperfect moments. In Unbroken, you will read the story of a woman who shed the clothes of herself and unlimitedly, letting go for God to take the wheel.

The Amplified Version of 1 Corinthians 10:13 says that,

"No temptation [regardless of its source] has overtaken or enticed you that is not common to human experience [nor is any temptation unusual or beyond human resistance], but God is faithful [to His word—He is compassionate and trustworthy], and He will not let you be tempted beyond your ability [to resist], but along with the temptation He [has in the past and is now and] will [always] provide the way out as well, so that you will be able to endure it [without yielding, and will overcome temptation with joy]."

Unbroken; A Mother-Daughter Journey of Resilience, Faith and Courage will become a second bible to rekindle the hope and resistance that many people need to endure and overcome their trials. It will make people grow a type of faith that allows them to trust God to prove Himself in their circumstances.

Above all, Unbroken holds a type of vulnerability in storytelling. One that is unafraid, unashamed and relentless in giving, for others to grow in faith and strength. For so long, this has been an untold story. However, by sharing Unbroken now, Dr. Egli has invested in her all, including Natalia. Unbroken is a way of saying that there is no going back anymore. Unbroken is here and Amen!

Oyindamola Shoola

Author of
Heartbeat | To Bee a Honey | The Silence We Eat | But Here You Are

Egli Colón Stephens, Ed.D.

INTRODUCTION

In all of my schooling in the United States, I was never exposed to Latino writers. The only literature I was mandated to read was about stories and people I could not identify with. I struggled to see myself, or my peers represented in the pages, but I never complained or questioned my teachers. I come from a culture where often children are silenced and to question an adult is considered disrespectful, so, I did not. I was just thankful to have crossed from the English Language Learners classes (ELL) to mainstream classes.

I was always under the impression that I had to check my Hispanic heritage at the door of my classroom and pick it up as I exited when it should have been the contrary. Celebrating and incorporating our heritage should have been part of the learning process of our history, but I did not want to offend my teachers in any way. The books we read reflected them and the administration of the school, but where were our voices? These books were not reflective of my experience, the immigrant experience. I grew up with the false illusion that Latinos weren't writers, until an eighth grade bilingual class at Walt Whitman Junior High School in Brooklyn, when I came across the Spanish version of *Don Quijote de la Mancha* by Miguel Cervantes Saavedra. Completely captivated by this book, I devoured it in a few days. *Don Quijote de la Mancha* was the first book I ever read and could not put down.

Upon discovering Latino literature in my late twenties as a young inner-city middle and high school teacher, I desired to expose my students to the work of writers of color, giving them the opportunities I did not receive. Writers such as Julia Alvarez, Esmeralda Santiago, Sandra Cisneros, Isabel Allende, Gabriel García Márquez, Pablo Neruda, Junot Díaz, and many others transported my students and me, giving us wings to fly each time we visited our local library and bookstores for their readings. Though it was never my intention to follow in their footsteps, when God gives me a command, I follow it.

Unbroken: A Mother-Daughter Journey of Resilience, Faith and Courage came to me first with the title, Co-Parenting with God. It came like a whisper; God's whisper and a strong conviction saying: *"Tell your story and share where I have brought you from. Tell people around the world that dreams don't have expiration dates.* Write your book." I never imagined that I would write a book or become an author, but this story has nudged me for years. It has woken me up from my sleep and many times, kept me awake at night. This story found me and I am honoring this calling by sharing my journey and my daughter's journey.

I was on a British Airways flight, 33,000 feet up in the air on my way to London to complete a doctoral fellowship in Interfaith and Inter-Religious Dialogue at the University of Oxford. Being a divorcee and single mom, I had already given up on my dream of studying abroad when this opportunity came along in 2005. Feeling flustered by this random experience, I started writing in my journal while on the plane.

I wrote endlessly, not once imagining it would unfold in this way. It began as a story I was writing for single moms, sharing my experiences about allowing myself to dream while seeking God's guidance, finding the courage to walk away from a troubled marriage, protecting my daughter from the outcomes of my hurt.

All of these, while focusing on being a magnificent mom to my healthy baby girl whom I did not expect to become critically ill at age twelve, when I also faced health challenges.

God had a different plan, a divine plan for what we now call Unbroken. *Uno propone y Dios dispone.* I believe I covered more than what I had intended. Here, you will find a God at work, making the impossible possible, creating a way where there was no way.

Unbroken will rekindle your hope and faith in humanity. Earth angels surrounded us and at times came to our rescue and prayed for us when we could not even pray for ourselves. You will find the power of community in action and how we became stronger than ever by walking through fire. In Unbroken, I don't hold back, I dig into memory and bring you to the source of this unwavering faith in my DNA, inherited by my grandparents. I take you to our humble beginnings in Santiago, Dominican Republic and even dare to incorporate some of my mother tongue, *Español*, here and there.

Through the process of birthing Unbroken, I learned to be still and trust God's timing. *El tiempo de Dios es perfecto.* The journals and documents I have compiled over the years look like a huge patched quilt. It has taken cutting and pasting hundreds of pages, letting go of many, writing, rewriting, renaming the book, searching through bins of pictures and learning to weave this journey creatively. I now understand why it has taken me thirteen years to put it into a book form. I needed a re-birth. I needed to be delivered, and these are not life events but a process that requires time. We have been healed not just physically but emotionally, mentally and spiritually.

For so long I would go back year after year hoping I could unbury this manuscript, go through my journal entries and put it in the book you are now holding, but it was so raw and excruciatingly painful, I could not get past page one without falling apart. It was not until 2014 that I permitted myself to remember that the storm was over. *You are safe Egli*, and I was able to dive into it.

Unbroken remains raw but hopeful. We take you to the battlefield to journey with us. Vulnerable and unashamed, I discovered a strength I never knew I had. I learned to endure, to be present for and with the one I love. I became one with my daughter during her darkest times and through her, I discovered that with faith in God, the human spirit is unbreakable. I learned to surrender to God. I learned to let life unfold and trust the process.

Thank You God, for placing our feet on solid ground and giving us the strength to come this far - for us to see where You have brought us from. The process has been cathartic, but through it, I discovered I was born to be a storyteller. I was born to write and I will do so until my last breath.

Egli Colón Stephens, Ed.D.

PART 1

Egli Colón Stephens, Ed.D.

CHAPTER 1
BIRTH OF AN UNWAVERING FAITH

Do not be anxious about anything, but in every situation, by prayer and petition, with thanksgiving, present your requests to God.
   - Philippians 4:6

Be faithful in small things because it is in them that your strength lies.
   - Mother Teresa

Before I knew of God, I knew God. I could not quote any Scriptures, but I knew deep in my heart and soul that there was a power higher than myself drawing me close. I must have been about seven years old when I first felt my heart sinking, missing my parents who separately emigrated to Puerto Rico and New York City in search of a better life, from the Dominican Republic.

Remembering the last image I had of Papi, I was about two years old when he left, and about seven years old when Mami left. They could no longer withstand the economic uncertainty and stagnant wages of our country as difficult as it was for them to leave their little girl and the island they were so enamored with.

Though my soul felt the sadness and despair of their absence, my spirit drew closer to prayer as I heard the echo of Mami's voice over my aunt's who tucked me into bed every night. "*Santo ángel*

Egli at 3 years old, posing with her favorite doll - a gift from her dad.

de mi guarda, dulce compañía, no me desampares ni de noche ni de día. Con Dios me acuesto, con Dios me levanto, en el nombre del Padre, del Hijo y del Espíritu Santo." I kissed my crossed fingers and recited "*Amen*" after gesturing the sign of the cross. I am the product of devout Catholic grandparents that prayed with me and for me way before I was born. There's no doubt in my mind that my grandmothers' devotion had a lot to do with my spiritual formation. Their devotion planted the seed of faith in my heart and it has

Egli at 10 years old, posing in front of her uncle's motorcycle, showing off a new dress her mom made her and brought from the U.S.

grown deeper as I have matured spiritually.

Leónidas and Ana Escolatica were my grandmothers. Ana Escolatica was Papi's mom. She was known to all as Colacita, but to my brother and me, she was Nana. They were both leaders of our local church, Santa Clara, in Santiago, Dominican Republic and were highly respected in our *barrio* for their selfless hearts and service to our community. Nana was the *curandera* and the *comadrona* of *el barrio*. She delivered babies and accompanied many as they took their last breath. In my eyes, she was a miracle worker. She prayed over the sick and without any medical training or tools was able to snap joints back into place with her bare hands. I remember our home was always heavily trafficked as injured people came in and out, and women also came for herbal remedies for their feminine issues.

She had the gift of helping people transition from life to death as well as welcoming a new life into the world. She was often called to pray over the dying when our deacon, Juan Gabriel, was not around.

For as long as I can remember, the priest was only present on Sundays to celebrate mass, but the deacon, the elderly ladies and the youth group ran our small church. Nana held the hands of the dying until their last breath, and then prepared them for the ceremonial burial, while the families sobbed outside the room. Most of our funerals were held at home. Only the wealthy and the well-established held their funerals en la *funeraria*.

Nana always left a big dress out on a chair to put over her nightgown in the event anyone came knocking at our door in the middle of the night for help.

She led prayer services, Good Friday processions and counseled the afflicted but was also the kind of lady no one messed around with. She took nonsense from no one. Nana was also wise, strong, determined and loved me with a kind of love unlike any other I have known.

I was Nana's little helper when I was not in school and people showed up for healing and counseling. As God's children, she strongly believed that we all had the power to heal one another in the Name of Jesus. She taught me to pray over people just like she did.

"*Ven Egli, estira tus manos y pídele a Dios con mucha fé que lo cure y le de descanso.*"

She never charged a cent, but once better, people gifted her with what they could afford to show their gratitude, a chicken for stew, a rooster, avocados, mangos or whatever crops they were growing in their backyard.

I enjoyed being around both of my grandmothers. They were each witty, and I saw them both as having supernatural powers. Although they were very different in character, their devotion and dependence on God left a lasting impression on me.

Egli at twelve years old "fresh off the boat."

When it was time for my First Communion, I knew all of my Catechism prayers thanks to my grandmothers. I was accompanying them to every traditional function that is customary of my Dominican culture and faith: wakes, funerals, rosary recitals, processions, *novenas, hora santas, nueve días, cumple mes y cumpleaños*. I was that inquisitive child seeking protection by their side, but also drawn to them and the comfort I found in prayer.

Nana's skills and prayerful spirit left such an impression on me that thirty-five years after her death, she is still very present in my daily life. I now understand that I was seeking a deeper intimacy with my Creator, or perhaps, my Creator was seeking me.

The only consistency in my life has been prayer. My

faith and spirituality have sustained me, and I would dare say, my faith has saved me. I have felt the presence of a silent, mysterious companion guiding and protecting me throughout my life. During the years of my parents' absence, I felt parented by my Heavenly Father. In the aftermath of my divorce, I knew my Heavenly Father could make me whole again and step in to help co-parent my daughter. I am convinced that amazing things happen when we pray for our children and with our children.

My grandmothers demonstrated devotion and taught me that I was not alone in navigating this sometimes scary world. They taught me to embrace the mystery of the unknown, ask for God's help, rely on prayer at all times, listen to God's whisper and take action. They taught me to seek stillness and silence because it is in the silence of our hearts that God speaks to us. They taught me to trust my gut and to believe that the human spirit is unbreakable when grounded in faith. They modeled that as long as we are breathing, we can bounce back from whatever life throws at us. They showed me how to show up for life, do my best, and let God do the rest. In a nutshell, they showed me what it truly means to surrender and trust that God would make a way out of no way.

I was about nine years old when my aunt Rafaela, Mami's second oldest sister and my primary caregiver, moved her three teenage children and me to my maternal grandparents' house. Every morning I was awakened by the sounds of roosters, our church's bells ringing at 6:00 a.m. and my grandparents chanting prayers.

My maternal grandmother, Leonidas, was not the most affectionate but was a woman of deep faith and prayer. She would nudge my grandfather, Miguel and in a firm but sleepy voice say, *"despiértate Miguel, vamos a rezar."*

Our rooms were divided by a paper-thin wall made out of plywood that did not reach the tin roof. The bed I shared with my aunt Rafaela was right against their wall, and I could hear every prayer. *Abuela* would initiate by saying, *"En el nombre del Padre, del Hijo y del Espiritu Santo, Amen."* I envisioned these words followed by the gestures of the sign of the cross.

I could smell the scent of the candle wax taking over our little wooden home as they prayed the rosary. As dawn approached, I laid in bed in the room next to theirs, taking it all in while falling in and out of my sleep. Prayer and devotion was something they could not start their day without.

They concluded their devotional time together by chanting the prayer of St. Francis back and forth. This prayer was my alarm clock and how I knew it was time to get ready for school. Despite them being long gone, I am still reminded that I am an instrument of peace. I can still hear the echo of their voices in my head chanting St. Francis' prayer:

Señor,
hazme un instrumento de tu paz:
donde haya odio, que yo ponga el amor,
donde haya ofensa, que yo ponga el perdón;
donde haya discordia, que yo ponga la unión;
donde haya error, que yo ponga la verdad;
donde haya duda, que yo ponga la fe;
donde haya desesperación, que yo ponga la esperanza;
donde haya tinieblas, que yo ponga la luz;
donde haya tristeza, que yo ponga alegría.

Señor,
haz que yo busque:
consolar y no ser consolado,
comprender y no ser comprendido,
amar y no ser amado.

Porque:

dando es como se recibe,
olvidándose de sí es como uno se encuentra,
perdonando es como se recibe el perdón,
y muriendo es como se resucita a la vida.

Their faith is what taught me where to go for comfort and refuge. Each time I closed my eyes, I connected to the purest and most sacred power I knew existed within me, my Holy Father.

Mother's Day, Circa 1976, Santiago, Dominican Republic posing in front of Egli's maternal grandparents humble home with family.

Egli Colón Stephens, Ed.D.

"I AM BECAUSE OF THESE WOMEN."

Egli's aunts and mother. L-R Aunts Mercedes, "Mecho," Rafaela "Faela," and Mami, Obdulia "Lula," the youngest of them all.

Egli's paternal grandmother "Nana," Ana Escolatica Colón. We all called her Colacita.

Egli at five years old, standing next to her maternal grandmother, Leónidas.

CHAPTER 2
A CHRISTMAS EVE MIRACLE

It is my pleasure to tell you about the miraculous signs and wonders that the Most High God performed for me.
- Daniel 4:2

Daughter, a beautiful creation... handmade by God, placed in the arms of a woman to rise, love, nurture, and treasure as a friend.
- Anonymous

I may not be certain about some things in life, but the one thing I am sure of is that I was born to be Natalia's mom.

I spent the first couple of months after her birth in awe and disbelief that I had given birth to such a beautiful and perfect being. She is my masterpiece, God's masterpiece, the best of me and the role I am most proud of.

***

My pregnancy was complicated, it was high-risk, and I bled until my sixth month, often being rushed to the hospital.

It was Christmas Eve of 1994. Natalia's dad and I were expected at my parents' house for *Noche Buena* dinner in Brooklyn. The night before, I had been out shopping with my mom in preparation for our big dinner, getting special Christmas plates and matching décor. All was set for Christmas Eve the next day, and the pernil had been marinating in Mami's fridge.

The day I had so much anticipated arrived, and I got up bright and early to go to the hair salon. Dominican hair salons are known for their crowded shops and popularity in New York City. They do an excellent job for a very reasonable price, but most times, appointments are not honored and the wait seemed like an eternity.

Though I was there early, the salon was packed just as I predicted. However, I insisted on waiting for Nilsa, my favorite hairstylist. I sat in a quiet corner to eat the healthy snack and orange juice I picked from the bodega on my way to the salon when suddenly, I felt a strong urge to urinate and rushed to the restroom. It was unusual that in my first trimester I was peeing so often. As I squatted down, I noticed a gush of blood come out and I yelled in panic. Immediately, everyone at the salon came running in to see what happened.

Nilsa rushed over to me, lead me to a back room near

the restroom and laid me down on a massage table while her mom, Minerva called an ambulance. I was frantic and began thinking the worst. From the looks on everyone's face, they were also thinking miscarriage.

As we waited for the ambulance to arrive, there was a mixture of silent moments as well as moments where they each shared advice.

"Nilsa put her legs up! This happened to my cousin, and it worked." A client shouted.

I knew that vaginal bleeding in pregnancy was dangerous and time was of the essence. When the ambulance finally arrived, I was rushed into the ambulance on a stretcher. The sirens cleared the way. I was anxious riding in the ambulance with no one there to offer me comfort. Everyone was doing their last minute Christmas shopping and my family could not be reached.

I was eight weeks pregnant and already in love with my unborn child. I was fighting to remain calm, so I closed my eyes and prayed for the safety of my unborn child.

Upon arriving at the hospital, I became overwhelmed by seeing the number of patients waiting to be seen at the short-staffed St. John's Hospital on Christmas Eve.

I was hemorrhaging and with the amount of blood the EMS paramedics witnessed, they were expecting the worst. "Miscarriages are very common amongst first-time moms in the early stages of their pregnancies, but we need to run some tests to confirm it." The nurse said.

Seeing my *comadre* Francis, Natalia's godmother and my cousin, Danelsy was comforting. They left shortly after to prepare their Christmas dinner and a few hours later, Natalia's dad was reached and immediately came to be by my side.

As I laid there on a stretcher against the wall in the hallway, alongside others, a nurse came to draw my blood. A few hours later, I was finally transferred into a curtained area, making it more private for my examination.

I felt hopeless as my nerves escalated. No one said a word, but I was holding onto some hope, while simultaneously thinking the worst. The body language and facial expression of some of the medical personnel were distant and cold.

Were they wondering how to give me the worst news expectant parents could hear? On Christmas Eve?

I was petrified when a gush of blood squirted out, staining the sheets and the physician's white jacket, as he inserted the cold speculum. At that moment, I lost all hope.

The stained sheets were removed, and I was put back out in the hallway to wait. I was shaking and the fear of the unknown crept on me as I struggled to catch my breath. There was still no explanations, but a blank look on their faces said so much.

Why was I not in the maternity ward, but instead laying here on a stretcher against a wall, in the hallway?

Finally, I was transferred to the maternity ward for an ultrasound. It had to be confirmed that I had an empty womb before I was sent home. Miraculously, we saw a very active fetus jumping from side to side with a strong heartbeat. "You got one active basketball player or a dancer in there jumping around, you are still very pregnant." The medical resident said.

I was in disbelief. This was my Christmas miracle, my answered prayer, and my gift from God. I wanted to jump with joy and hug this unknown Latina medical resident who performed my exam. Noticing she was wearing a small pendant of *El Divino Niño*, I felt baby Jesus had come alive and I knew my daughter was here to stay, a pivotal moment in my walk with Christ.

I was sent home and instructed to remain on bed rest.

Drained from the stressful day at the hospital, we canceled dinner at my parents and decided to stay home. Natalia's dad and I had a quiet Christmas and spoke about baby names. It seemed impossible to come up with any boy names and eventually, agreed on Natalia meaning, Christmas Day.

Though Natalia was born in mid-July, her name is appropriate as she came fully alive that Christmas Eve.

At my second trimester follow-up, I was referred for an ultrasound because of the occasional spotting that continued. I was thrilled hearing my baby's strong beating heart. I reclined comfortably on the stretcher, allowing the technician to get the best image of my baby while I listened attentively to her heartbeat.

She rolled the sonogram device on my belly repeatedly, zooming in and out, and shooting images as if she was looking for abnormalities. I got scared.

"Is there something wrong ma'am?" I asked.

"I am sorry. I am unable to discuss this with you. Your obstetrician will give you all of the results and answer any questions you may have."

"But I am not scheduled to see my doctor for another week," I pleaded.

"Are you aware that you were having twins?"

Before I had any time to get excited, she quickly said, "One of the amniotic sacs is empty, I am sorry to say. But please, you cannot say I disclosed this information to you. I can lose my job for this."

I left the hospital devastatingly confused. This news was bittersweet. I walked down Queens Boulevard to the bus stop, holding my growing belly and feeling grateful for the baby I was still carrying.

It is no wonder family and friends have told me not to get attached to the baby during the first and second trimesters. I guess these things are common.

I fell in love with my baby from the moment the home pregnancy test showed positive and knew in my heart we were going to be just fine.

I was given all the printed images of the sonogram,

and although there was plenty of ambiguity, I was rejoicing in how beautifully my baby was forming and developing.

In the weeks to come, I was never given a clear explanation, not even after I was switched to Long Island Jewish Medical Center. Their only comment was, "It is possible to miscarry a baby when carrying fraternal twins because of their development in separate amniotic sacs."

Knowing this did not bring one of the babies back, but it explained the hemorrhaging at the hair salon on Christmas Eve. On the day I received my Christmas miracle, Natalia, my other baby went to heaven.

For most of my pregnancy I carried the weight of this news, and though I was primarily focused on carrying my child full term, I was seeking answers and exploring the possibilities of another miracle.

What if a baby is hiding behind Natalia and I receive this surprise during labor? In recounting this, I realize I never mourned that loss. I dismissed it and focused on keeping my child alive. Some things will remain a mystery, and sometimes we have to be okay with that.

The remainder of the pregnancy was a pure delight and like every nesting mom, I prepared for her debut by carefully choosing her layette and nursery.

My belly was so big that sleeping at night became difficult during my last trimester. That hot summer my hobby became cooking in my underwear and eating all through the night while I slept during the day. I was trying to regain the weight lost during the morning sickness and took the term that a pregnant woman eats for two, literally. Before I knew it, I could rest a plate on my huge belly. I cherished the movements in my belly, as I ate my savory food.

A few nights before my due date, I woke up in the middle of the night to urinate when I noticed a bloody discharge. Since my scare at the hair salon, I developed a habit of looking inside the toilet before flushing.

What is this?! I have no contractions, and my water has not broken!

In total panic, I ran back to my bedroom. Natalia's dad and I called our obstetrician, and he instructed us to hurry to the hospital. Though the hospital was only 30 minutes from our home, at that moment, it felt like an eternity.

It was still dark when we arrived at the hospital at five in the morning and, though my obstetrician had not yet come, the attending physician on call examined me. I was nervous when they explained they had to insert a thin wire for direct contact with her head to make sure she was not in distress.

"The wire may cause a minor scratch on the baby's scalp, but don't be alarmed. Everything will be okay, and she will be safe." The nurse assured me. "It is a protocol that we inform you so that you do not worry if you see a scratch on the baby's head."

This is not how I imagined my labor to be. I thought I would be worry free after all I have experienced.

Shortly after, my labor was induced with drugs. The baby was beginning to show signs of distress. I could hear the rain and thunder outside, but I was no longer afraid. I had grown in my faith and knew that God was protecting us.

Though the contractions were occurring, my obstetrician felt it was safer to rupture my water sac and accelerate the labor. Before I knew it, my legs were floating in the water that had nurtured my baby for nine months.

I began to feel the sharp pains brought on by the Pitocin. The pain was so intense and stung so bad that I felt like my back was going to crack. I had not experienced abdominal contractions, but as Natalia was pushing through, I became delirious from the pain. I gasped for air as her head ripped through my insides. I thought I was going to die!

Her dad put on his scrubs and coached my labor as we welcomed our first born.

"Breathe, Egli. Remember to wait for the contraction, and then breathe as you learned in Lamaze class." He said.

Not long after, I demanded an epidural. The Demerol was not easing the pain and I could no longer bear it after so many hours in labor.

All that time in labor, I had dilated only three centimeters and the umbilical cord was beginning to wrap around the baby's neck.

"Push harder," my doctor instructed.

"We may need to take you into the operating room and prep you for a C-section."

Hearing this gave me the strength to focus. I was determined to push hard and bring my child to life. Life had prepared me to push through, and it was preparing me for the experience ahead with her.

On the twenty-third hour, my daughter entered the world weighing seven pounds, three ounces and measuring twenty and a half inches long. Natalia Cecilia Harris was born on a stormy Tuesday, July 18th, 1995, at 3:30 in the morning; a beautiful baby girl of ivory complexion and green eyes. She is the spitting image of her Nana.

Her dad held her for a moment and then gently placed her on my chest. She felt warm with cheeks as soft as a rose petal. I was instantly in love, calling her by her name. I kissed her and blessed her. I thanked God for the greatest gift of my life. Immediately, she latched on to my breast as if knowing the sweet, life-giving nectar that was coming from her mom. This was the beginning of a nurturing relationship and an exchange of spirits. At that moment, Natalia gave me life.

She has infused me with a different kind of power and since then, has filled my life with so much purpose. I am grateful for my daughter and pray for the little angel that went to heaven that Christmas Eve of 1994.

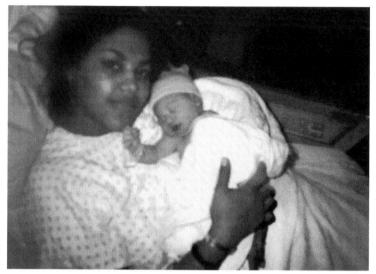

Natalia's debut, minutes after being born.

CHAPTER 3
CHILDREN DO NOT LISTEN TO WHAT WE SAY, THEY WATCH WHAT WE DO

Start Children off on the way they should go, and even when they are old they will not turn from it.
    - Proverbs 22:6

Children are educated by what the grown-up is and not by his talk.
    - Carl Jung

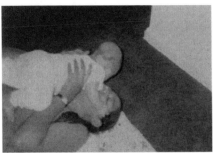

Egli playing with Natalia at two months old.

Natalia's first year of life filled me with many mixed emotions. As the first child, grandchild and niece in both families, she was welcomed like a royal child. She brought us all immeasurable joy, but deep inside, I had concerns about not being able to give her the life I had envisioned. I was afraid that my adolescent, tumultuous marriage to her dad was not going to last and I was right.

I prayed for a miracle. I really wanted our marriage to work and respectively sought out pastoral and marriage counseling.

I prayed so much with the hope that God would salvage our marriage, and indeed He listened to what my heart was genuinely saying.

Save me, dear Lord. Fix my marriage or give me the strength I need to leave. Give me a clean slate.

I knew the kind of example I wanted to be for my daughter. Therefore, I decided to walk away from my marriage.

Our children do not listen to what we say; they watch their surroundings and what we do. Therefore, it was at that moment when I decided to take back my power.

***

I was seven months pregnant when I knew in my heart my marriage was not going to work, but I was too scared and embarrassed about what people would say about me leaving. I had a feeling in my gut even before we married but decided to ignore all the signs. I was vulnerable and believed things would change.

When we fail to listen to our internal GPS or God's whisper, we miss His message, give in to fear, self-doubt and instead, follow the negative voices. I take full responsibility for not honoring my intuition.

Though I was filled with anguish, I wanted to honor the commitment I made to my husband, knowing that the covenant of marriage was intended by God to be a lifelong fruitful relationship.

I was beginning to feel like a failure, believing I was not capable of holding my family together and giving my daughter a home. This continued until the day my therapist said these words to me that would ring in my ears for years to come.

"You don't need to come to see me anymore. I suggest you seek legal advice. There's absolutely nothing wrong with you psychologically; you have realistic expectations of a wife."

I was saddened to be dismissed and felt paralyzed, but those words also validated me. I was not crazy, neither was I unreasonable.

That day I drove home and sat in my car while watching the sunset from our driveway. Tears rolled down my eyes as I thought about how to leave. I felt defeated.

It has been over two decades since that 1996 August afternoon, and just like a *mariposa*, I flew away. Natalia was only thirteen months old and I knew then, it would be my final attempt to leave.

As I pushed back tears, I reminded myself that it was time to fly, *"vuela mariposa, vuela alto." This is the opportunity you have been asking God for.*

"*Mírame* Egli," my mother said to me while I drifted into despair. "*Levanta la cabeza mi hija, pa'lante, tienes que luchar.*"

"Keep your head up high; pick yourself up for your daughter's sake. You did all you could," Mami said. We went home and were welcomed by my parents with open arms. I reassured myself that I tried my best and I never looked back.

I knew that life as a single parent was going to be challenging, and I made a conscious decision to protect my daughter from myself. Protect her from the hurt, the anger, and the bitterness I felt over my broken dreams. I was careful to watch what I said about her father in her presence, and my family did the same.

In time, God answered my prayers, and I learned to forgive and let go of the resentment I felt. I sought out professional help and relied on God and my community of faith to help me grow. I experienced God's healing and restoration, and trusted in His justice and divine plan for my life. I can confidently say that the remarkable young woman that my daughter has become and the woman I am today, are proof that my prayers have been answered.

Treating Natalia's father with dignity and modeling respect even during difficult times, have been vital in cultivating a healthy, trustworthy and loving relationship with my daughter.

Providing an atmosphere of peace, stability, and joy in our home was my priority, and I had to become that, first. As Natalia got older, she planned her time with her dad, and I am glad to say that she has never had to choose between the two of us. The marriage did not work, but Natalia has not been a fatherless daughter.

I take pride knowing that I never tarnished her father's image, and this is how I know that God has been my faithful companion and co-parent on this journey. I learned to let go, and in turn, the trajectory of our lives changed.

Plant the seed of love, faith, and forgiveness, and it will harvest.

As a result of planting these seeds in my daughter's heart, she has grown to be a very well- adjusted young adult with the necessary tools to navigate life and overcome obstacles.

I walked out of the marriage on faith with twelve dollars in my back pocket, my dignity, my daughter and the support of my loving family. Today, I am content to have created the life I envisioned for us, and there is no greater satisfaction than being responsible for the life we create for ourselves.

Natalia and Egli at different stages. They are one heartbeat.

CHAPTER 4
WHATEVER WE SURRENDER TO THE DIVINE WILL BE TRANSFORMED

Therefore do not worry about tomorrow, for tomorrow will worry about itself. Each day has enough trouble of its own.
  - Matthew 6:34

We have to pray with our eyes on God, not on the difficulties.
  - Oswald Chambers

Natalia was turning three and getting ready for nursery school when we moved out of my parent's home. It was hard for my parents to see us go, but they respected my decision.

Natalia at two years old with open arms, ready to embrace what the world has in store for her.

My mom cared for Natalia while I worked and restored myself again. Their love and tender care restored my soul, and I was ready to spread my wings again.

When I realized my marriage was falling apart, I was convinced that a big house in the suburbs was not what makes a home. Collecting home catalogs, magazines and creating vision boards became my new hobby while I saved up for our move. I had a vision for our new home, and I yearned to bring that vision to life.

Eager to embark on our new journey, I focused on creating a sanctuary in our new two-bedroom apartment in Bay Ridge, Brooklyn. I wanted our new home to be infused with creative corners for prayer and meditation, with the freedom to play and allow our minds to run free.

Like me, Natalia was drawn to prayer and a contemplative life. She grew up in church and this was part of who she was and continues to be, therefore, prayer and meditation in our home were just an extension of our faith. She often initiated by taking me by the hand to sit in her quiet corner to meditate with her. We had embraced our new home and neighborhood; creating structure and routines in our new lives.

When we moved, Natalia was still in her terrible twos, a stage I thought would last forever. She was a handful and a very feisty little girl. I learned how to depend on God and regularly sought His guidance, especially during her many tantrums when I felt helpless.

Many times I found myself losing control and directing my frustrations toward her. I had to choose my words and walk away for a moment, consciously. I learned to praise her and give her affirmations instead, realizing I was the one who was out of control.

The daily pressures of life had me depleted, causing my negative energy to surface. Juggling graduate school, work, and my motherly duties had me exhausted and feeling defeated. Through therapy, self-care, learning to ask for help and God's grace, I became a better parent, learning to be present and giving her the attention she was seeking from me.

I remember a time when Natalia was having a meltdown, and I could not figure out how to soothe her. I threw myself on the floor and began to have a tantrum with her.

Is being a single mom something I will not learn to do on my own? Help me, dear God, I don't know what else to do.

"You look crazy mommy; you are crazy." She yelled.

I honestly felt like I was losing my mind, but God's grace saved me, and I soon began to feel His presence in her tender touch, her laughter, her innocence and her dependence on me.

By far, parenting is the hardest and most challenging task I have ever done, and I commend those with multiple children. This is the most selfless, unrecognized, unconditional and sacrificial human-kind of love I have ever known, but it has also pushed me to grow deeper and expanded my capacity to love selflessly.

Gospel music had always spoken to my soul. I depended on it during those difficult days when I often did not have the words to pray. Marvin Sapp's Gospel song, "Never Would Have Made It" became my anthem every time I overcame a challenging situation. My eyes still well up every time I hear this song. I made it.

Asking for Jesus' help in co-parenting came naturally, as I grew closer to God in prayer. I leaned on Him during desperate times and released my burdens for Him to carry. Choosing to remain graceful was difficult, but I received peace in knowing I was not alone. I felt God breathe new life in me, shifting my thoughts from fear to hope.

I am blessed and highly favored. *Yo soy una mujer bendecida, yo soy ricamente favorecida"* These were the affirming words I would repeat in front of the mirror and that I genuinely believed as a daughter of the Most High.

Surrendering requires courage and is not for the faint of heart. It doesn't mean giving up; it means releasing our burdens to God and allowing Him to transform our situations. It means less of me and more of Christ, allowing the divine to reside in me. It means letting go of control while not permitting my fears, obsessions, judgments, and anxieties to make a home in my mind; trusting that His plan is bigger and better than my own. Surrendering has become my way of life and my most reliable parenting tool.

In my faith and devotion to my Creator, I have found the strength to surrender the burdens and tensions of daily living instead of carrying them with me. I noticed they were debilitating and manifesting themselves in my body through aches and pains. The practices of daily silent meditation, prayer, Scripture reading, exercise, play, good nutrition, hydration, rest, and continued learning have helped me live a more centered life and freed me from unnecessary tension.

My breakdowns turned into breakthroughs and God transformed my situation into one I would have never imagined.

As I matured and evolved, I went from survival mode to taking action on my dreams. My personal and professional life are both informed and transformed by my spiritual life. I have learned to listen to God's whispers, gain wisdom from Scriptures and trust in Him wholeheartedly.

I left my career in healthcare administration when Natalia started Pre-K and went into education, seeking deeper professional and personal satisfaction but also to accommodate motherhood. I was halfway through my first graduate school semester in counseling at New York University and found myself having to withdraw. Between Natalia's transitioning from nursery to Pre-K, and my adjusting to a new career, I felt myself falling apart, and my focus became being present for my daughter. Withdrawing from grad school was one of the hardest decisions I had to make. I felt defeated and quitting had never been an option, but I had to prioritize.

Natalia was seven years old when I went back to graduate school and my comeback blew my mind away. It unfolded so organically. Halfway through my master's program, I was accepted into a doctorate program. In maintaining a 4.0 GPA, I was offered a partial scholarship and the opportunity to study a semester abroad at the University of Oxford in the United Kingdom.

At times I felt guilty and conflicted being a working mom while attending graduate school, but this time, I was not giving up. This time I was going to show my daughter to never give up on her dreams. I wanted to show her what it meant to be relentless.

Juggling school, work and time with Natalia was challenging, but deep inside, I knew I was laying a solid foundation for the two of us. Sacrifice is not forever, I would often tell myself to keep me going. Many times I denied her the playground because of my commitment to my education, and my determination to succeed. Natalia was patient and understood that I had work to do and the times I had to bring her to class was never an issue for her. My classroom was her playground.

"Professor, would it be okay if I skipped all the grades and came to college?" She asked.

At the time she was in third grade and was always happy to assist the professor in handing out assignments. She was well behaved and adjusted well to the circumstances.

Natalia was also very busy. Managing her extracurricular activities was like having a second job. I enrolled her in ballet at the age of three, swimming at the age of four, pottery at five, horseback riding at the age of eight, ski camp in Vermont during the winter recesses and her dad enrolled her on a basketball team. She also attended the Brooklyn Children's Museum with her Nana weekly and was given piano lessons by the same music teacher that taught her grandmother.

As a single parent on a budget, I do not know how I made all of this happen, but I am a firm believer that when we live within our means, operate from a place of abundance, give generously to those in need, God multiplies our resources. My mom would often tell me that my money has an elastic band; I stretch it. *"¡Mi hija, a ti si te rinde el dinero, creo que tiene elástico!"*

These memories are all fresh in our minds, and I am proud to have instilled in her to finish what she starts, teaching her discipline and perseverance. Natalia would often tell others, "My mom is so much fun." It was difficult to ever see myself as a fun parent when I was also the disciplinarian and felt more like a drill sergeant. So many times I felt enveloped with fear and despair, but somehow, always pushed through and trusted in God's promises for our lives. As a woman of faith, I learned to shift from a mentality of fear to one of strength, hope, and trust.

I often rejoice in the life I have created for my daughter and marvel at the wonders of God's presence in our lives. Everything I had envisioned became a reality and I am delighted with the daughter I have raised. She truly blows my mind.

She doesn't remember her father and me living together and has been able to accept the circumstances for what they are. He has been a present and consistent father in her life, giving her the love, provision and attention every daughter deserves. I believe that because of our dedication to her, she became a well-rounded young lady who learned to navigate both worlds.

Egli and Natalia's Christmas card 2005.

Natalia at 12 years old, almost Egli's height and already fitting into her shoes.

Natalia and Egli.

PART 2

Egli Colón Stephens, Ed.D.

CHAPTER 5
LIFE AS WE KNEW IT

He heals the brokenhearted and binds up their wounds.
  - **Psalm 147:3**

No one ever told me that grief felt so like fear.
  - **C.S. Lewis**

Cherry blossoms were blooming everywhere in New York City on this spring day of April 14, 2008. I was recuperating from a major surgery, so this time it was Mami who drove us to pick up Natalia from school. I had been holding on to the hope of having more children, but after several attempts to preserve my womb, I lost my battle. The constant hemorrhaging became so debilitating; my family pleaded that I have my uterus removed rather than risk my life.

"Egli, no puedes arriesgar tu vida. ¿Piensas dejar a Natalia huérfana?"

I would never forget the day my sister Jenny looked into my eyes and said, "If you ever want to have another child, I would carry the baby for you, sis. I can't stand seeing you like this anymore. You cannot continue to risk your life for the possibility of one day having another child when you don't even have a prospect. Natalia depends on you."

Freezing, under layers of white blankets, my eyes fixed on the pints of blood being transfused before the removal of the benign tumors growing inside and outside of my uterus, the idea of my sister offering to be my surrogate filled me with hope and gratitude. She was only twenty-two years old.

Papi stood on the side of the bed, while Mami rubbed my legs and prayed.

"Que se haga la voluntad de Dios mi hija. Tu no déjaras de ser mujer si te sacan todo eso que ya no te sirve."

It was difficult accepting that my uterus was no longer going to serve me and my dreams of having more children were shattered. A part of me died that day.

The chronic anemia caused by constant hemorrhaging made it difficult to breathe and walk while still having to function and provide for my daughter. I was exhausted on so many levels. This condition had robbed me of living a normal life.

Suddenly, it all made sense as I reflected on the words of wisdom repeated to me on that day. Thinking about my precious daughter as the last pint of blood was being transfused, I asked my family to call in the surgeon.

"Dr. Wilcox, I have decided to go on with the hysterectomy instead. I do not want to risk anymore."

"That makes sense Egli; I was respecting your wishes although the procedure was not guaranteed. We will be taking you into the operating room soon."

I was given papers to sign. My family became elated upon hearing my decision; they witnessed my health deteriorate one procedure after the other. They kissed me and helped push the stretcher into the operating room; I waved goodbye as they blew kisses and reassured me we would see each other soon.

Although I woke up in excruciating pain, the surgery was a success.

***

For two weeks, Natalia complained about pain on her right knee. I was still recuperating and like most Latinos, believing it was the cure for everything, I applied Vicks Vapor Rub. Even after giving her Ibuprofen, she was still in pain. I did not notice any bruising or swelling, so I thought that as an active twelve-year-old involved in many extracurricular activities this was all part of growing pains. Her dad is about 6'7," and I am pretty tall as well. That same week I received a note from the school nurse suggesting I should take Natalia to the doctor because of her persistent visits.

It is unusual of Natalia.

I immediately scheduled an appointment with the orthopedic as per the pediatrician's recommendation.

We arrived at Natalia's school a few minutes before dismissal and double parked in front of the school's building. Finding parking in Harlem was nearly impossible. I worked across the street from her school but was on sick leave recovering.

We headed out to the orthopedic in our old neighborhood in Bay Ridge.

Natalia was asked to put on a gown and escorted to the X-ray room before seeing the physician. This was a state of the art facility and the X-rays were done quickly. I was still in shock but looking back now, I imagine the room was white. Natalia sat on the examining table and I sat on a chair opposite her. A tall, white man wearing a lab coat walked into the room. He introduced himself and without a pause, put the X-rays on a reflecting white light on the wall and pointed out to the femur on her right leg blurting out, "She has a tumor. It is about the size of a lime and I am 99.9% sure that it is malignant."

And just like that, the world as we knew it was turned upside down and inside out. Within minutes, our lives forever changed. I was stunned, hoping it was a bad dream. Realizing my daughter was in the room, I could not understand why I was not given the option to let her stay in the waiting room so, she would not hear this terrible news.

I wanted to scream and pushed back tears; my heart was pounding out of my chest. Natalia, being the bright girl she has always been understood the horrifying discovery.

These things don't happen to people like me.

But that is not where it ended; he continued to disclose what felt like atomic bombs exploding in my chest.

"She has a tumor on her right distal femur the size of a lime, you see? Right there." He pointed on the screen.

"I am 99.9% sure it is malignant. This kind of cancer is called Osteosarcoma and it takes about a year or two to treat if caught on time, which I think we did. I will refer you to the two best physicians that treat this kind of cancer in New York City. Let us hope they take your insurance."

It was 6:20 p.m. when he left us in the examination

room to make some phone calls. I followed him, but could not keep up. I was still limping from the pains of my surgery, holding on to my abdomen. I walked over to my mom instead and collapsed in her arms. I cried so hard I feared my incision would pop open.

"Mami el doctor dice que Natalia tiene un tumor en la pierna y el está casi seguro que es cancer."

Mami had no immediate reaction; perhaps the shock paralyzed her. She stood up and walked with me to Natalia.

"The doctor is crazy or probably seeing things. It is not possible to make a quick diagnosis just by looking at an image. We have been here for less than an hour." She said in Spanish.

I repeated the doctor's findings to her but was still in denial.

"Eso fue la imagen de una mariposita que iba pasando cuando le hicieron los rayos equis, no te preocupes mi hija. Estoy segura que eso fue lo que el doctor vió, tranquila."

"Really mom? A butterfly passing by while the X-rays were being taken? Couldn't you come up with a better lie?" Natalia said. "Good one mom."

I went out to find the doctor.

Though Natalia did not shed a tear, I knew she was upset. As the young girl she was, she seemed to be angrier at the doctor demanding we canceled her trip to Barbados which was supposed to happen in the following week.

The doctor was on the phone in a nearby room trying to get a hold of a specialist in the city to begin treating Natalia's condition.

"Time is of the essence; she needs to be treated soon."

He was unable to get a hold of anyone since it was past office hours and gave me their direct phone numbers to contact them the next morning.

Natalia could not grasp the severity of the situation,

and neither could I. I was in disbelief but had to keep it together. I had to remain strong for the both of us and immediately went into survival mode, absorbing all the information and strategizing a plan. Saving my daughter was my only option.

I needed the doctor to repeat the diagnosis in my mother's presence even though Mami's understanding of the English Language was limited.

Suddenly, I felt as if we were in a movie. Everything was in slow motion, including the words coming out of the doctor's mouth. My stomach turned, and an intense sense of panic swept over me as he repeated, "There is a hairline fracture on your daughter's leg. We would have to amputate her leg to prevent the cancer from spreading if she happens to break that leg."

"I can't take her home like this; she is too fragile!" I finally exploded.

"Go to the pharmacy across the street. Here's a prescription for stronger pain medication and crutches. Make sure she doesn't break that leg! Call these numbers in the morning. These are the two physicians that treat her condition. Hopefully, they take your insurance." He said without hesitation and avoiding any eye contact.

Natalia was still trying to negotiate to go on her trip the following week. "I will be very careful and make sure I don't break my leg in Barbados, doctor."

"You cannot get on a plane. You cannot travel. You need to stay put." He said in a firm voice.

She mumbled a couple of words under her breath stating that she was still going. She was entitled to grieve in any way she pleased, so I remained silent.

I was ready to put my daughter in a bubble. I wanted to carry my 110 pounds, 5'10" twelve-year-old out of there in my arms. I wanted to move people out of her way. I was confused. I was angry. I felt helpless and dismissed. I did not know what else to say or do. I could not believe the doctor had done *all* he could.

What does he mean there's nothing else he can do?! Couldn't he call an ambulance or hospitalize her? Isn't this life-threatening?!

We slowly found our way out of the office. I felt disoriented and for a while forgot where I was. I wanted to become my daughter's crutches and wrapped her arm around my shoulders, allowing her to put her weight on me as she hopped out. Mami grabbed the other arm reminding me how delicate I still was.

"Tu no puedes hacer fuerza mi hija."

I did not care that I shouldn't be lifting her. None of that mattered. Saving my daughter's life was all I could think about.

We walked to the pharmacy across the street to fill the prescriptions.

"Leave me alone. I can walk on my own. I am still going on my trip with my dad and Nana!"

Natalia was in denial and disappointed. Mami and I looked at each other, feeling her pain and confusion.

We respected her wishes and allowed her to cross the street without our assistance. Mami walked beside her, and I walked behind her, making sure she did not fall or miss a step. Impulsively, I would extend my arms in case she fell.

Mami and I avoided eye contact as best we could, when all we wanted to do was embrace each other and weep for our little girl. The uncertainty of the road ahead of us was daunting.

We crossed Third Avenue and went into the pharmacy. Mami sat Natalia down on a chair by the counter. As I walked towards the pharmacist, I was trying to come up with a plan to have my daughter admitted into the hospital. I was scared.

The doctor prescribed adult size crutches for Natalia. She was three months away from her thirteenth birthday and had reached puberty before the diagnosis. The orthopedic explained that the tumor developed after a rapid growth spurt. She was a size $8^{1/2}$ in shoes at the beginning of the school year, and by April she was already a size 10. Her arms and legs were long too, and I often found myself buying new clothes and sending her old ones to her cousins in the Dominican Republic.

I was desperate as we waited for her prescription to be filled. Mami continued to avoid eye contact, preventing a break down between both of us.

When we got home, Natalia insisted that we work on her science project due the following day. She was convinced that she could go on with life as usual and that the doctor was exaggerating.

She went into the kitchen with her new crutches like a pro and asked me to help her.

"I don't want to show up to school without my project, mommy, so come on."

I looked at her and just followed her orders. We created a cell membrane with jello, clay, grapefruit and other stuff I can't remember. The pain medication started to kick in, and she slowly dozed off after she was done with her project. She made her way to the room; I helped her put on her pajamas and tucked her in. I was relieved when she fell asleep. I wanted to do the same to wake up the next day and say this was all a horrible nightmare. I felt like burying my head in the sand but knew I could not.

Something deep within told me that I had to seek immediate help. I knew in my heart that my daughter was not well although she looked terrific and was as stubborn

Natalia playing tricks with her crutches.

as a mule. I sat on the edge of her bed, caressing her face as I watched her sleep peacefully for about an hour or so. My heart was sinking. As she slept, I asked God to please watch over her, to let this be a false alarm and let it be a benign tumor. I asked God to guide me and show me the way. Covering my mouth as I sobbed, I knelt in front of her bed, stretched my hands over her and pleaded to God. "Lord Jesus, please please, please, don't take my daughter away from me. Help me. I need you. I'm desperate. I don't know where to turn to; please come to my rescue in my midnight hour."

I stayed there for a few minutes and wept as I gently caressed her leg and prayed for healing.

I had been on bed rest for the past couple of weeks recovering and began to feel uncomfortable in that position. I slowly got up holding on to her bed and went to the kitchen. I passed the phone, looked at it and decided to pick it up. I thought to myself, what do I have to lose? I started calling the offices of the doctors we had been referred to. It was past midnight. I knew no one was going to answer, but I wanted my messages to be the first ones they retrieved when they got in the office. I cleared my throat and composed myself. I left clear messages about my daughter's condition and asked to be called back to set up an appointment. I spoke with urgency and confidence. I prayed internally that whoever listened to the messages in the morning would call me back with some guidance. I hung up the phone and started to walk and pray around the house as everyone else slept. I did not want to wake up anyone as I tiptoed on our old hardwood floors and went back into Natalia's room.

I watched Natalia sleep some more and decided to do some research on the computer.

I need to be well informed and prepared to go into the offices of the physicians when they call back.

I was determined to show up with my daughter if

they did not call me back in the morning. I forgot what the condition was called and reached out for the paper where the orthopedic had written it. He spoke about it with ease and familiarity, although it seemed like a foreign language to me.

I was hesitant to explore the web but decided to Google Osteosarcoma anyway. I closed my eyes after pressing the Enter button and opened them, slowly. The more I read, the less I understood. Or maybe, I did not want to understand. I went to YouTube hoping that a video would shed light into this darkness we were in, when a video of a leg reconstruction popped up by one of the physicians we had been referred to, I played it and immediately became nauseous and light headed.

I can't even imagine my daughter going through anything near any of this. I shut off the computer without logging out.

Natalia continued to sleep peacefully. I tried to lie next to her and could not stop watching her breathe in and out. I was afraid of closing my eyes. A feeling of helplessness overcame me. Morning did not come soon enough; this night was the longest of my life. It was as if time had frozen. I was tossing and turning on her bed and did not want to wake her. The fear of falling asleep with her, knocking her leg and breaking it, paralyzed me.

How could this have happened? How did I become afraid of touching and breaking my daughter? Was I dreaming about this?

I was restless. It was impossible to fall asleep, not even in the bed directly across from her. Forcing myself to close my eyes, I thought, the *sunrise will bring new hope.* I needed to hold on to that 1% possibility of Natalia being cancer free. I needed this for my sanity.

As dawn was breaking, I continued to pray for answers. *I need to move faster than this darn cancer that was beginning to take over my daughter's life, my life. We are stronger than this!*

Natalia slept past her wake-up time, and I had no intentions of sending her to school. Her Nana and I planned on tag teaming; she would consult with her physicians and I with mine. I was unable to sleep or eat, but Mami insisted I should eat something.

It was 9:00 a.m., but I still had not heard from anyone. *Why isn't anyone calling me, damn it?!* I was waiting to hear from her pediatrician but never did. I was delusional. *Was he not calling me because of fear I would blame him for not detecting the tumor sooner?*

Natalia's attitude remained the same as yesterday; she was upset that we did not wake her for school. "We need to make sure your leg is fine first," I explained. She was zooming through the house with her new pair of crutches as my heart hung from a thread watching her do new tricks she was beginning to learn.

"Ay Dios mío ayúdame" This became my constant prayer as I would try to keep up with her.

Though our home was filled with suspense, my parents remained calm in our presence. I was looking out the window holding my head in despair when my dad walked in.

Placing his hands on my shoulders, he said, *"Tranquila mi niña que todo está en las manos de Dios."* I needed to hear those words, those words that brought me so much comfort.

Everything is indeed in God's hands.

I was finally able to settle Natalia on the couch but continued to pace around aimlessly.

Okay, I am going to take a shower. No! What if I miss a call from a doctor's office? I scratched my head and peeled the skin from my lips, not being able to make up my mind about anything.

Wait? What if the phone is off the hook? I checked a couple of times to make sure it was working.

Okay, it is working. I am going to take a shower now. Feeling disoriented, I walked out of the shower.
Did I just take a shower? Yes, I did. I think. Okay Egli, time to get dressed.
"Put on my pants: now my shirt: and now my shoes." I said out loud; this was my way of staying on track, of staying present.

It is 10:15 a.m. now. The phone rings. "Finally!" I ran to answer, "Hello?" My voice trembled.

"Good morning, this is Shelly. I am calling from Memorial Sloan Kettering Hospital. You left us a voicemail about your daughter. Are you available to bring her this afternoon at 2:00 p.m.?" She continued, "Bring a copy of her birth certificate, proof of address, a photo ID and insurance card, please."

"Yes, yes, we will be there." I replied with a broken voice. "What is your address?" By the time I hung up the phone, I was on autopilot, ready to go.

I was ready to take over and I was the one taking the wheel from here. Walking to get my car, I was finally able to mourn my daughter's condition. I knew this was the only time I had to release some of the anxiety that had built up and doing it in front of my daughter was not an option.

"Do you know something I don't?" Natalia would ask me. "Stop crying; I am not dying mommy!"

The ride to the hospital was a quiet one for Mami and me, while Natalia skipped from one radio station to the next, singing along. When we pulled in front of the hospital, I froze for a second, realizing what our new normal had become.

A young bald girl was coming out of a yellow cab with whom I imagined was her mom. I was shocked. I had only seen the St. Jude's hospital commercial with bald children and the kids on the pediatric floor when I worked at Brooklyn Hospital, but there was a disconnection, a disassociation. I never imagined this affecting us directly. I froze. It took me a while to drive away. I stared at them and then drove once I looked at the clock.

"That is not going to be us." I said to myself.

I dropped off Mami and Natalia in front of the hospital and went to park the car. I put the car in a parking lot, paying an expensive fee and did not even try looking for parking in the streets of Manhattan. I walked over to the hospital about two blocks away.

I noticed people in wheelchairs and some women with headscarves on, coming in and out of the hospital and in the vicinity. I was seeing the world through a different lens and noticing things I usually never noticed. I could not believe so many people were being affected by this cruel disease; I still thought we were exempt.

I met Natalia and Mami in the registration area. We registered and then proceeded to do the X-rays and a CAT scan of the affected area as instructed, before seeing the oncology team.

Prayer has been my lifeline for as long as I can remember and this time was no exception. I kept holding on to all I had at this time, my deep faith.

Egli Colón Stephens, Ed.D.

CHAPTER 6
PRAYING MY WAY THROUGH THIS

For we live by faith, not by sight.
   - **2 Corinthians 5:7**

Although the world is full of suffering, it is full also of the overcoming of it.
   - **Helen Keller**

Entering the doors of Memorial Sloan Kettering Cancer Center was like checking into a five-star hotel, except this was a five-star battlefield. We were fighting for our lives. The orchids that always surrounded us were a reminder of how precious and delicate life was and the friendly personnel felt like ambassadors of hope with their warm smiles and helpful dispositions. They must know that by the time one makes it there, they are distraught with their diagnosis. Every ounce of courtesy, care and attention is much appreciated.

We were prepared for the worst when we went for a second opinion on that Tuesday afternoon, April 15, 2008. Although Natalia's case was familiar to them, it was foreign to me. Nothing made sense. After a CAT scan, X-rays and blood work, we met with the oncology team and were told to return the next day for more tests. Again, the doctors' voices echoed each other. I was stuck in a nightmare I could not wake up from and refused to listen to their speculations. Their voices bounced off my head; I became deaf to their conclusions. The knot in my stomach was suffocating me. Clenching to every ounce of hope and faith, I wanted to believe this tumor was benign.

I remember that day as if it were yesterday; it was 6:30 in the evening when the orthopedic surgeon, the pediatric oncologist and his team confirmed to Natalia, Mami and me, what the physician from the day before had suspected. I thought I was going to collapse in that consultation room. All of them were 99.9% sure that my daughter had Osteosarcoma, a form of bone cancer.

"We are going to perform an MRI and more tests tomorrow and will schedule her for a biopsy this week. Everything indicates that the tumor is malignant." The pediatric oncologist explained.

Feeling in and out of consciousness, I immediately broke into a cold sweat. I was gasping for air, drowning in a pool of despair and desperation.

They were very patient with us. I kept asking the same questions over and over, expecting different answers. I could not understand why such a harsh diagnosis without a biopsy was possible. *How can they expect me to grasp all of this?* It all came at me with such force like a volcano erupting.

"Patients with this condition usually need a leg reconstruction and about twenty-five cycles of chemotherapy." The Doctor continued.

The medical team never withheld any medical information from Natalia. They were direct and involved her in every step of her care.

The Child Life Specialist on-site at Sloan Kettering, Evan, as well as my friend Aissa, who is also a Child Life Specialist often explained her condition to her through play and understandable language. They both made sure she was on the same page, but Natalia, barely a teen, was often a step ahead of them. She wanted nothing to be hidden from her. Her level of maturity and courage impresses me to this day.

Although we were asked to go home, I asked that she remain overnight. We were denied the request after all the tests were completed. I could not believe they were sending us home and I demanded we stay!

"Did you not hear my daughter's condition? Why can't we stay?" I forcefully asked the head nurse.

"We have to be back here early in the morning." I insisted as I pointed at all the empty beds in the clinic.

"This is a day pediatric hospital," she repeated. Her words fell on deaf ears. "We don't keep patients here overnight."

"Let me speak to your supervisor; I want to be transferred to another floor and have my daughter admitted!"

I paced up and down the hallway like a mad woman looking to speak to someone else. My daughter needed to be hospitalized. I feared my daughter's shattering her leg like that of a porcelain doll. Her crutches became her new toy, my worst nightmare. The nurse understood my grief and in an overly compassionate manner, convinced me to go home.

I felt helpless and defeated; mentally, emotionally and physically exhausted. Mami and I carefully took our *vidrio de Belen* home. Our Natalia was as fragile as porcelain, and I was like a zombie as I walked on York Avenue to 66 Street; I was collapsing. My breath, faint, was like a flatline monitor. I was inconsolable and choking with the weight of the news.

***

The following day, we returned for Natalia's prep exams before the biopsy the next day. The doctors thoroughly explained the procedures and planned the next year of treatments.

It was early evening, still daylight when we rode back home from the prep exams. Natalia turned on the radio. Mami called home to let Jenny and Papi know we were on the way and to wait for us outside to help bring Natalia in.

When we arrived at my parents' apartment, it was filled with caring neighbors and friends from church who had heard the bad news. They prayed with us and for us. They helped us carry our grief.

The testing, retesting and events of the past forty-eight hours had been the most chaotic and horrific of my life. I silently prayed everywhere; I offered myself as a walking prayer.

"Hold us tight Lord and never let us go," was my prayer and that, He did. I felt God's presence with us, getting us through each step. I knew that we were in the hands of the divine, but I still could not shake off the pain of my daughter being sick. I got the strength to endure through my prayer and faith that God had our backs.

I was sleepless after putting Natalia to sleep that night. What had transpired and what was ahead of us played in my head like a scratched record. My mind was going 200 miles per hour and I could not keep still. I decided to send out a massive email to all my contacts asking everyone to join in prayer for my daughter's healing. I believe in the power of unity. I believe in the power of community and praying for one another. For as long as I can remember, writing has been my way of coping and processing information, so I spent the remainder of the night writing to ask for one of the most valuable gifts: Prayer.

April 17, 2008, 3:22 a.m.
Subject: Urgent Request to Pray For Natalia's Health

If I am reaching out to you, it is because, in one way or another you have touched our lives. In the past forty-eight hours our lives have been impacted drastically and we can't seem to wrap our minds around it. We need God's help; we need your prayers for Natalia's healing.

On Monday evening, my mom and I took Natalia to an Orthopedic Doctor because she had been complaining of a knee-leg pain for the past couple of weeks. During this visit, X-rays were taken, but I did not think they were going to reveal any abnormalities. Natalia had not fallen or bruised her leg in any way. We all thought she was going through growing pains, after all, she has been growing fast for a twelve-year-old!

What I thought was going to be a routine checkup for my peace of mind turned out to be the worst diagnosis ever. I was just told that my daughter has cancer.

My heart is sinking. I feel that the world as we knew it has fallen apart. I am staying as strong as I can because she needs me and I am trusting that the God that has gotten me out of darkness before will get us through this.

The chest scan done today was clear; there are no tumors on the chest. I am still waiting to hear about the bone scan done tonight. Today again, we checked into the pediatric hospital and spent most of the day running tests. It was a long and draining day filled with uncertainties. Tomorrow will be even more intense.

I am trying to stay in the "now," and breathe.

Natalia is sleeping peacefully by my side with an IV on her arm and her leg is on a brace.

In almost two hours, 5:30 a.m., we have to check into the hospital again for a five-hour surgery, where a biopsy will be done. If the tumor is malignant they will immediately insert a Mediport: a catheter that connects the port to a vein through which drugs can be injected (chemotherapy), blood samples can be drawn many times, usually with less discomfort for the patient than a more typical "needle stick."

Hopefully, this will not be our case, but even if the tumor is benign, she needs to have a bigger operation in three months to repair and replace the bone with some metal.

La esperanza es lo último que se pierde, I'll hold on to hope. It is all I have!

I am kindly asking and begging you to please, please keep hoping and praying for Natalia's healing.

In faith and hope,
Egli

***

Natalia woke up cheerful and full of optimism, despite knowing it was the morning of her biopsy. We arrived at the hospital at the crack of dawn and prayed for God's will to be done. Her Nana and dad met us there. My parents and my younger sister Jennifer were also there. We held on to the hope that the tumor was not going to be malignant, although the physicians knew what to expect. They advised that it was procedural to perform a bone biopsy before beginning chemotherapy. Natalia was told that if she woke up with a lump by her chest and bandage, it meant she had cancer. It meant they had inserted the Mediport for easier access to a vein during chemotherapy.

I was still in denial. *Why are they telling her all of this?! Let us get there or not!*

We prayed together and as we assisted in rolling the stretcher into the operating room, we held back our tears. Natalia, being silly and hopeful, smiled at us and told us she would be right back. To her, this all seemed like a big adventure.

"Bye-bye," she said as she waved.

I asked the orthopedic surgeon if she could remove the tumor and do the leg reconstruction right then and there if she found the tumor to be cancerous. I did not want Natalia returning to the operating room again three months later.

She said, "It is not that simple; we need to do further studies of the bone."

At that moment, I found myself bargaining and giving the experts suggestions and all kinds of alternatives on how to proceed. I was desperate. My heart was being ripped out of my chest. It was hard to entrust my most precious jewel to the hands of a surgeon I had just met and her entourage of apprentices.

"Please do your best, she is all I got." I said this as they walked away.

I wanted to hold her hands and pray with her but did not want to delay the procedure anymore. As Natalia was wheeled away, I silently blessed her and prayed. Lord, into your hands, I commit my daughter and everyone who is operating on her, may their hands be blessed: Amen.

Shortly after Natalia was taken in, a nurse came over.

"I will be in the operating room; I will come out periodically to keep you informed. Hold on to this pager; the procedure will take about five hours, when it goes off, you can go see your daughter in the recovery room." She said.

I held the device and begged her to please come out as often as possible to keep us informed.

"Where's the chapel?" I asked.

"Straight ahead," she pointed.

"You will find me there," I replied.

I did not want to speak to anyone or be spoken to unless it was some medical personnel with information about my daughter. I wanted to be one in spirit with her and felt the best place to do that would be in the chapel. My family stayed in the waiting area and respected my wishes.

***

As I pushed open the doors of the small chapel, I felt a sense of relief in this sacred space and all by myself. I walked up to the altar and knelt.

"I don't know what to say, God." I prayed.

I felt depleted. I looked around at the Tiffany glass windows that surrounded me and decided to get up and sit on a pew.

"I know you can hear me. God, I need a miracle." I said, as I looked up to the ceiling in hopes of seeing angels descend. I was at my lowest, still holding on to what I knew had sustained me all my life: My deep faith in God.

"I feel empty God. I am offering you my empty heart, my presence here, my uncertainty, let this be my prayer to you today."

I prayed as I lay in a fetal position on the pew holding on to the device the nurse had given me.

My mind wandered off; I kept visualizing my daughter laying on a table, in a cold operating room just a few feet away from me. The thought of her being cut open, poked, probed, pale, helpless, intubated and unconscious was driving me insane. I sat up, then laid back down and began to talk to God again.

"I praised You when things were well, and I will continue to praise You. You have never left me, and I know You are not going to leave me now. Please give me Your peace, Lord that surpasses all understanding. Help me to surrender to You."

I kept looking around, expecting to hear a voice, but I knew the answer to my prayer was going to be found in my heart and the direction of my next steps.

Hours had passed and the nurse came to the chapel a couple of times to tell me that Natalia was doing well and that the procedure will soon be completed. I went back to the pew and again found myself in a fetal position talking to God.

"God, are You listening to me? I want You to know that I trust You and this is not going to make me lose faith in You. I will pray my way out of this tragedy if I have to, but we are doing this together." Soon, I slowly dozed off.

The pager started beeping and I woke up in a state of panic; disoriented. For a moment, I thought I was home, but sadly remembered where I was. I found the door and soon saw other family members. A couple of minutes later, the nurse came to us.

"Ms. Colón, your daughter is in the recovery room now, she is sleeping. The orthopedic surgeon would like to speak to you before you see Natalia. Please follow me."

My knees weakened, my stomach turned.

As I sat on a chair in a small cozy room, nicely furnished with white orchids and a box of tissues on the table, I thought to myself, "This is the room they bring the family when they have to tell them the bad news." Before the orthopedic surgeon opened her mouth, I knew what she was going to say.

"Natalia's tumor was malignant. I inserted the Mediport on her chest. We need to begin chemotherapy next week before removing the tumor and reconstructing her leg in about three months."

They had warned me, but I was numb hearing this final confirmation.

"I need to see my daughter," I replied.

"She is still not awake." The orthopedic surgeon said and continued to share what happened during this long procedure and what to expect next. I was so angry and disappointed to hear this. could not help but think about the road ahead and the pain my little girl would have to endure.

"Please let me see my daughter," I asked again.

The rest of the family was in the waiting room and my friend Aissa was with me, she never left my side and asked all the right questions as she took notes. She knew I was distraught and could not process any more information. I could only wear my mommy hat at that moment and hurt for my daughter. I just wanted to see her.

I begged the orthopedic surgeon to let me see my daughter. I promised I would not wake her up.

"I have to be by her side when she wakes up," I repeated.

I was escorted to a room full of dead-looking patients recently out of the operating room, some attached to breathing machines. I looked everywhere and quickly spotted my little girl still sleeping in the recovery room. She had a couple of IV lines but was not hooked to any machines. I leaned over her and kissed her softly on the cheek. I stood there watching her for over an hour, then, sat in a chair next to her bed. I stretched my arms over her, caressed her head and thanked God for getting her out of the operating room safely.

A few minutes later, Natalia woke up as she felt my hands caress her face. I was hoping my tender touch would be my healing prayer. I was lost for words, drowning in my grief but pushing tears back. She had forbidden us to cry.

She opened her eyes, winked a few times and went straight for her chest. I watched in silence and suspense. She pulled the layers of the white sheets that covered her, looked down at the bandage, and touched the hard bump and without words we both nodded our heads in disbelief. She frowned as she closed her eyes.

My mom and sister had grown impatient and somehow convinced the nurses to let them in. I heard the curtains roll, but I did not move. Natalia and I were holding each other in a silent embrace when they joined in.

"We are going to get through this together," Jenny exclaimed cheerfully.

As the day went by, family and friends visited bringing words of encouragement. Natalia's entourage took over the entire waiting room all day. There was deep grief among us, as well as profound hope. We all agreed not to cry in her presence and she did not want it any other way.

It was the end of the day and my comadre Patzy who knew me so well, knew I needed to cry. She rushed me to the restroom. She held me as I collapsed on the stall floor and wept inconsolably.

"You will get through this Egli," she whispered.

"Why not me? Why can't it be me to go through this pain?!"

I imagined an hour had gone by. Patzy helped me up to wash my face and gain composure.

Natalia spent the night at the hospital. I stayed by her side. My parents were concerned about me spending the night sitting on a chair considering my recent surgery, but I refused to leave my daughter's side.

I remember that night being long, scary, extremely quiet, cold and lonely. I was the only relative allowed to stay that evening. I spent the night tippy toeing back and forth to get heated sheets for Natalia. I wanted to make sure she was warm and comfortable while she slept. I kept Natalia's curtains closed. I wanted to shield my daughter and I was restless. Periodically, I would put my fingers under her nostrils to make sure she was still breathing, afraid that she would stop.

Is this happening? Are we really at Memorial Sloan Kettering surrounded by people dying of cancer?

There were moments I could not contain el llanto, and I would walk with my hands firmly against my mouth. I did not want my daughter to hear me sobbing.

The thoughts of days, weeks, months, years ahead, made the present unbearable and it was at that moment when the meditative lessons that I had been teaching about staying present to one's breath became a challenge. The unknown was paralyzing. To be present, my mantra became "One breath at a time and one step at a time."

At that moment while in the hospital's hallway, I leaned against the wall and slowly slid to the hospital floor.

God, please give me the strength to get through the night.

I picked myself up and put one foot in front of the other following the square tiles leading back to the recovery room. Every breath and step I took was intentional.

Dawn came and the new day brought new hope. The surgeons began their rounds and everything remained the same. The change of shift and the loud noise from the team woke up Natalia. They replaced her IV and she went back to sleep. It was very early when Mami and Jenny arrived.

"*No dormí la noche entera pensando en tu sufrimiento mi hija.*" Mami said.

The thought of the pain I was enduring kept Mami starring at the ceiling all night. She could not wait until the morning to be by our side.

***

It was ten in the morning when Bill, the principal of the school where I worked came to visit, along with Father Parkes, the school's president and Eva, my friend, who was also the school's social worker. I was invited to a mass taking place at the small chapel in the school which I attended regularly. I did not decline. I knew that my faith and community was going to give me the strength to go on. I asked Natalia if she would be fine with me going.

"Go ahead mommy; I will be fine."

This was the first time I was seeing the sunlight since I went in with my daughter a day prior.

Father Parkes flagged down a yellow cab on York Avenue while Eva and Bill held me. The sunshine blinded me as I looked up at the blue sky.

How can the sun still shine when my world is so cloudy?

The ride to the school on 116 Street and Park Avenue was quick and quiet. I sat by the window and opened it so that the air could refresh my face.

When I entered the chapel, most of my colleagues were there. We all mourned in solidarity. I sat next to my friend Gladys and I remember having a blank stare as Fr. Parkes celebrated mass, my mind often drifting to Natalia.

"*God, please nurture my starving soul with Your bread and wine. Please sustain us with Your body and blood.*" I prayed silently as I stretched my hands again to Fr. Parkes and asked to give me another Eucharist, to bring communion to my daughter.

I wept when mass ended. I cried as each co-worker came by to wish us well and rushed back to class. I felt embarrassed for being vulnerable, but I could not hold the tears back any longer. I mourned as if my daughter had died. I cried out of fear of the unknown, anger, frustration and desperation. I also cried out of exhaustion. After mass, they returned me to be by Natalia's side.

"Mommy, unless you know something I don't know, please don't cry. I am not going to die." Natalia said.

I could not help but ache for her and what was ahead. I knew the chemo treatments and operations were going to be brutal.

Natalia did well throughout the day and we were discharged by evening.

"All is set for Natalia to return on Monday to begin her first round of chemotherapy." Her nurse said when she came to check on Natalia.

We had a full house for the entire weekend. The family from Jersey and some of her classmates came to visit. Away from Natalia, we embraced each other in solidarity and wept quietly.

I buried my head in my *madrina's* chest and cried. I could not contain the grief when I saw her. My godmother loves me as one of her daughters and felt my pain. She embraced me and cried with me. This moment held an unspoken language, an embrace of sorrow. There were no words that could bring consolation.

Jenny had planned a fantastic weekend of fun and relaxation for Natalia. She invited some of Natalia's closest friends over and we bought ice cream, fudge, sprinkles, popcorn and all kinds of goodies to enjoy as they watched movies and hung out. It was a relief to have my younger sister entertain Natalia as I processed my grief with the adults and prepared myself for the week ahead. We needed to keep her distracted and enjoying some of the things she liked.

***

On Sunday we went to church as usual, except

this time Natalia was on a wheelchair. We could not believe that so much had happened in a week. Our small church community felt our pain; they were very supportive. Natalia had grown in this church where she did her First Communion, Confirmation and had become an altar server in this community of faith. During the service, the pastor, our friend Joe, called us to the altar to be anointed with oil and have everyone pray over us. We knew that the next day and every day after that, we would need to be strengthened by others, as a community's love has the power to heal the broken-hearted.

CHAPTER 7
READY FOR COMBAT

Put on the full armor of God, so that you can take your stand against the devil's schemes
    - **Ephesians 6:11**

It isn't the mountains ahead to climb that wear you out; it is the pebble in your shoe.
    - **Muhammad Ali**

Natalia was kept in the hospital two days after the biopsy and was sent home on Friday to enjoy the weekend. They scheduled her to return on Monday, April 21, 2008, to begin chemotherapy at 7:00 a.m.

Sunday evening, I packed her bag and set aside comfortable clothing, leaving everything ready. Since bathing had become such a big hassle for her, I helped her wrap a big garbage bag over her affected leg; put one leg in the shower and the other sticking out of the tub. Leaning against the wall, she would dry herself up, get into her pj's and go back to bed. I laid by her side.

I prayed and then asked, "Do you know what is going to happen tomorrow?"

"Of course I know mommy," she replied. "They have only explained it to us about a thousand times. Even before this was confirmed, they told us everything about it. Do you want me to explain it to you?"

Before I had a chance to respond, Natalia was already giving me details about the procedure.

"They are going to draw more blood and then connect an IV, or several IVs to the Mediport that is here on my chest.

"Right here, Mommy," she pointed at her chest. "This little thing here is my friend now. You know how much I hate to be stuck with needles and with this little thing, they don't have to poke me over and over again to find a vein."

I was astounded at how much she knew. She was so curious when the medical team would give her explicit explanations about the game plan.

"I am so impressed with how much you know and how brave you are Natalia."

Her gentle hands held my face as she said, "Mommy, I am going to be fine; trust me."

"How are *you* doing? You have not taken care of yourself this week." She continued.

I hugged her; I could not believe she was concerned about me in spite of everything she was going through. I held her close and caressed her head as I pushed back tears and whispered in her ear, "I love you. Get some sleep now; we have a long day tomorrow."

Within minutes she was asleep. I stayed up staring at the ceiling in despair until my body gave in and I fell asleep too.

***

The next morning the aroma of Mami's cafecito soothed my soul as I was trying to wake up from what I thought was a nightmare. I stayed in bed tossing and turning still half asleep.

When I opened my eyes and saw the brace on Natalia's leg and the crutches leaning against the wall, I remembered this was our new normal.

A river of emotions began to overwhelm me again. I grabbed my towel and ran towards the shower. My sister had given us her room and was sleeping on the couch. I needed to let it out; instead, I collapsed on my sister and cried uncontrollably as she held me and whispered, "Shhhhh, don't let Natalia hear you like this."

I was afraid to face the permanence of our situation. I tried covering my mouth as I buried my face against her stomach, but the sorrow came from so deep within that *el llanto* woke up Natalia and abruptly, she came hopping on one leg without her crutches.

I quickly sat up, wiped my face and ran over to hold her, afraid that she would fall. Mami ran from the kitchen when she saw her shadow and heard the stumping.

"What is going on, mommy?" "Why are you crying so loud?" Natalia asked.

"I am upset and scared," I said.

"Stop that mommy! You scared me; I thought something had happened to you."

This was a pivotal moment in this long process and I promised myself that it would be the last time she was going to see me cry. She sat on the couch with Jenny and I went into the shower to cry. I often found myself crying in the shower or alone in the car. Other times, I would hold it in.

You have to pull yourself together, Egli, I thought and grabbed my head to try and calm myself down.

***

"Have any of you had a cold, fever or rash in the past couple of days?" asked the clerk during registration.

Simultaneously and in sync, we responded, "No."

Natalia was given an admissions bracelet and we were directed to the waiting area. Protecting Natalia and the other patients being treated became our priority. We learned to volunteer our health status before being asked, and if any of us felt a cold coming on, we would put on a mask immediately.

Jenny was the buffer between Natalia, the medical team and me. She kept Natalia laughing, distracted, and involved in all kinds of fun activities in the hospital. Mami was the faithful UNO cards playmate. I was the observer and compulsive note-taker, questioning physicians and documenting everything in a personal medical chart that I created. I kept a binder with a list of her medications and did my research on the long and short-term side effects, manufacturers and reviews. I also wrote the name of every new medical personnel that treated her. As a previous Patient Advocate at Brooklyn Hospital, this all came naturally to me.

That Monday morning of April 21st, 2008 marked a beginning for us. I put on the full armor of God. As scared as I was, I decided to entrust my fears into the hands of the Lord and stay present for my girl.

No more tears, I am ready for combat.

Before the first treatment started, we met with her care team again in the pediatric oncologist's office. They examined her and explained the process as usual.

"How did my daughter get cancer? Did I do something wrong?" These were questions I continuously asked as if the past was going to change our present situation.

"Could I have done something to prevent this from happening? Do you think a fully organic diet could have prevented this? Did the use of the microwave give my daughter cancer?" I continued.

Though they must have thought I was losing my mind, they were very patient and answered all my questions.

Maybe there was something I could have done. I blamed myself and could not shake off the horrible sense of guilt.

"You are a good mom; we can tell you take good care of your daughter," The pediatric oncologist said.

"For the most part we eat everything organic, but sometimes I buy regular fruits and vegetables on sale and rinse them well. I keep a clean home and cook fresh meals every day." I continued.

The pediatric oncologist came over to me once again, "You have done nothing wrong. See this as bad luck. See it as being struck by lightning. Many kids get diagnosed with this kind of cancer in the United States."

"This doesn't make any sense; I don't believe in bad luck," I replied.

I insisted they should continue to do extensive research to help prevent this merciless disease from attacking innocent children.

"This is so unfair," I said as he nodded.

"I know, it is not fair. In the meantime, let us start her treatment and get her settled into a room in the Pediatric Day Hospital. Paulette, the Nurse Practitioner, will check on her periodically and I will see her at the end of the day before you go home."

The pediatric floor was bright and kid-friendly. There were clowns and musicians on the floor, distracting the kids from their misery. As we waited to get situated in a room, we met families who traveled from as far as Dubai for treatments.

In the midst of my tragedy, I felt blessed to be surrounded by family and friends. I felt blessed that we could go home every night. I could not imagine what it would feel like to be in a foreign country, alone, fighting for my child's life. Hearing other's success stories of overcoming this illness gave me comfort and strength in so many ways.

***

"Hi, I am Nurse Christina, you can call me Christie. I will be your nurse. Follow me to your room."

In the room we helped Natalia out of the wheelchair and into the bed. It was a small room with a large window and a view of the New York City skyline. Nurse Christie was comforting and optimistic. She explained the process and side effects as she hooked Natalia to the IVs infusion.

There was silence in the room, but Natalia had lots of questions.

"Is it going to hurt?" She asked.

"Not really," Christie replied. "You will get a little nauseous with this yellow chemo, but I will give you some medication for that."

Jenny, Mami and I looked at each other, still in disbelief. Natalia remained in bed for the first dose and Christie explained that there will be two doses.

Initially, Natalia was in good spirits, but as the week progressed, she became weaker and weaker, forcing her to stay in bed most days. By midweek the vomiting was so intense that she had to be sedated. She could never recall being carried out of bed or being put on the wheelchair every single day.

The first week was brutal. The side effects kicked Natalia's butt and we were also exhausted. This would become our daily routine for more than a year. We would check into the hospital at 7:00 a.m. and check out at 7:00 p.m. That same week, we began to see chunks of hair on her pillow and by the weekend, patches of her hair were gone. This process was ruthless and a constant reminder of the enemy that lived inside my daughter.

With every strand loss of her hair, my heart sank.

My daughter's rapid transformation was surreal. Right before my eyes, she became pale, lethargic and had bags under her eyes as if she had not slept in years. She had lost her appetite and was getting weaker by the day.

"God, give me Your strength. Help me to be as courageous as Natalia." I quietly prayed as I watched her sleep.

By Friday, we were discharged at five o'clock and instructed to bring her back if her condition worsened.

"If she develops a fever over the weekend, do not hesitate to bring her back to Urgent Care. If all goes well, come back on Monday for the second round."

We stormed out of there as fast as lightning desperate to leave the place I felt was eating my daughter alive.

We survived the weekend without any visits back to the hospital. We had hand sanitizer dispensers installed everywhere and asked visitors to refrain from kissing her. Though Natalia was in good spirits all weekend, she was weak and barely got out of bed.

Mami and I spent the entire weekend making nutritious meals with hopes of getting her to eat, but she rejected almost everything. It would break our hearts to see that her favorite dishes were no longer appealing.

"They make me nauseous, mommy," she would say, declining our offers.

Many times, she would get a craving and would

lose her appetite by the time we prepared the meal.

We were warned about infections because her immune system was weakening, so, that Sunday, we stayed home from church. Monday came fast and we were ready for combat again.

Cycle two, bring it on! Natalia needed three consecutive months of chemo before the removal of the tumor and the reconstruction of her leg, followed by more rounds of chemotherapy.

Week two was just as brutal. It is a blur. I was on autopilot and have very little recollection of it.

I had no time to return the many phone calls and emails received during those two horrendous weeks. My dear friend, Aissa, came up with the brilliant idea of setting up a blog through CaringBridge so that I did not have to worry about contacting everyone, individually.

This blog helped us connect with the outside world and gave us the opportunity to post updates and receive encouraging messages from friends and family. This became our bridge, our faithful companion in our almost two-year battle. It took me over five years to revisit those entries, but I am now ready to give you a raw glimpse of our darkest hours with the hopes that you too, can be strengthened.

We are overcomers!

The first entry to our journal is from Natalia. It was written about two weeks after the diagnosis. She was three months short from turning thirteen.

***

April 26, 2008, 5:01 p.m.

It is me, Natalia. As you probably already know, I was diagnosed with Osteosarcoma which is a malignant (cancerous) tumor that arises from the bone itself. I found out on Monday, April 14th, when my mom innocently took me to an orthopedic doctor because I was complaining of knee pain.

Who would have thought that from a simple pain, the doctor was going to tell me, I had cancer? Not me!

Before that day, I thought the pain was growing pains since I am so tall and active. But no, I had it all wrong. This, of course, has been very difficult for me, I am having a lot of ups and downs. I am hoping to get the hang of things soon. I am trying to keep my life the same as it was before I found out this news.

My family is getting through these terrible moments by sticking together. We are hanging in there.

Thank you for all the love and support.

Peace-Love-Strength,
Natalia

April 30, 2008, 12:24 a.m.
Day 17 on our road to recovery

Dear Soldiers,

    We are in combat. It is the middle of the night, and Natalia is sleeping by my side. We are now beginning day seventeen of this battle with cancer. I am feeling a little bit numb and overwhelmed.

    Natalia had a good day today in comparison to how chaotic things have been. She ate twenty-one grapes for breakfast and I spoon-fed her some chamomile tea with honey and lemon for lunch. She has lost most of her appetite since we started treatments. She no longer craves for the food she used to enjoy and sometimes when she does, by the time she gets it, which is really quick, she no longer wants it. I feel that each day, this enemy robs us more and more, but we will persevere. She asked for my mom's rice and beans and she ate a few teaspoons. She then asked for a homemade lemonade with lots of ice, and she drank it all for dinner. She was also craving Sushi, and Jenny took the B41 bus on Flatbush Avenue and went to Park Slope to get it for her. She rushed back on the dollar van, and Natalia only ate a few California rolls. I was a bit concerned with her eating raw fish, considering how weak her immune system is becoming, but I took the chance. Her little body is beginning to look so fragile, she hardly eats anything and it worries me.

    Life has not been the same since the diagnosis. Nothing tastes the same for me either. I sometimes eat out of obligation, but I am somehow blowing up, I am gaining weight. I no longer see the world as I used to. This all seems like a nightmare I can't wake up from. This is our new reality, and I am praying for acceptance. I am thinking in short sentences, I now see life in slow motion and can't come up with complex statements. This too shall pass.

There are so many mixed feelings; I don't even know where to begin to trace our steps for these past seventeen days. All we know is that we are going to get through this with a positive attitude. We are going to get through this with all the love from our family and friends. We are going to get through this with faith, hope and God by our side. Natalia's strength keeps me strong. Thank God for her innocence and simplicity.

Well, when she sleeps, I must also sleep, so it is time for me to go to bed. I never know how our days will go. I don't know if I will make it to bed tomorrow, but for now, I will stay in the present moment and at this present moment, I am lying next to her, breathing the air she exhales, like when she was a baby. When she exhales, I inhale her, when she inhales, I exhale with the hopes to infuse each other with the breath of life, the breath of God.

She sleeps peacefully. Good night *mi corazón*.

Mommy Egli

May 7, 2008, 12:09 a.m.
Day 24 on our road to recovery

Dear Soldiers,

Natalia just went to sleep in my arms, and I slowly slid out of bed to come to the computer and be with you through this journal. I am listening to India Arie's song, "This Too Shall Pass." I am so confident that this will pass and I am speaking it into existence. I know God can, and I know God will carry us through this. As I welcome this new day, I pray to my God to quiet my mind so that I can hear His voice whispering that this too shall pass.

It is not easy for me to stay present with all the suffering children we see at the hospital and everything else that goes around us, but I keep telling myself, "our story is different, our story will have a different ending." I try to be compassionate and sympathetic with all the other cancer patients we meet and their families, but I constantly remind Natalia and mostly myself, that our story will have a different ending. We need to put on our blindfolds daily and stay focused on our path. "We will finish strong."

Cancer did not just rob my daughter of her health, but it has affected other areas of our lives, like our finances. I can no longer return to work from my sick leave. I know that my place is with my girl and I know we will get through this. We are victorious and we will get through our challenges with determination and faith in God.

We got through cycle one of chemo triumphantly. The side effects kicked butt, but Natalia kicked harder. Her white blood cells dropped drastically last week and she had nothing in her body to fight back infections. Thank goodness she did not get any.

Last Thursday, when I took her for her checkup, her team of caregivers at the hospital were amazed that she had not been hospitalized with any infections, high fevers, mouth sores or any of the other side effects that accompany chemotherapy. Her team kept looking for her name on the list of patients admitted daily, but Natalia did not need to be hospitalized. Hooray! I am counting our little victories.

She has been in great spirits, singing, dancing on one leg, eating at all hours of the night, joking and playing dominoes with *Mami* and *Papi*.

Yesterday, we went for another checkup and she is doing great considering the circumstances. The white blood cells went up from 0.2 to 15.1. That is a fantastic improvement. She is also recovering back her weight. On Thursday, she was 104 pounds and yesterday she was 108 pounds with the bionic leg. We are on the battlefield, my friends. We are fighting hard, staying focused and keeping our eyes fixed on the final prize. Natalia is indeed on her way to recovery, although we have a long way to go.

Nothing can keep Natalia from dancing and singing. I don't want to crush her spirits, but she may kill me of a heart attack if she keeps dancing on one leg. The orthopedic surgeon gave her a lecture about hopping and dancing on one leg with or without crutches. Hopefully, she will stop putting herself at risk of breaking her already fragile leg.

On Monday, May 12th, 2008, almost a month since the initial diagnosis, we will begin three consecutive weeks of chemotherapy. We have been warned about the aggressive side effects. I can't imagine them being worse than during this first cycle. I don't even recognize my daughter anymore.

I found her in my parent's bathroom with my dad's clippers. She was shaving her head. She was beginning to have too many bald patches on her head and just got tired of finding bunches of curls on her pillow. I found her leaning against the sink with "Will," the hurt leg slightly raised. She corrected me when I tried to tell her to give me the bad leg to put on socks.

"Don't call it the bad leg mommy, I decided to name it Will, "Will get better, Will walk again," she said.

"Ok, I will call it Will from now on."

I was stunned when I walked into the bathroom and noticed she had parted her hair in three rows and was giving herself a Mohawk. I did not have the courage to keep watching her or even to ask her where she got the idea from. My eyes swelled up and I just walked away. Jenny was in the house and got her out of the bathroom. She sat her in a chair in the living room in front of the full body mirror outside her closet door. From there, Natalia indicated how she wanted her new haircut.

I am always afraid of giving my daughter too much time alone; sometimes, I just don't know what she may be up to.

This past Sunday, Natalia received her confirmation. We were afraid she was not going to make it to church, but she did. Her peaceful demeanor truly reflected the

After the side effects of the first round of chemotherapy, Natalia made the tough decision to shave off her hair to avoid waking up to patches of hair on her pillow.

Holy Spirit that lives within her.

Hasta pronto,
Mommy Egli

May 11, 2008, 11:29 a.m.
Day 28 on our road to recovery

Dear Soldiers,

Mother's Day just ended thirty minutes ago. I stood in front of the computer for over thirty minutes, just trying to sort out my feelings and figure out what to write. This was a very unusual Mother's Day for me. I don't even know how to put into words all the mixed emotions felt on this day. I am privileged to be a mom and what an honor to have been chosen to be Natalia's mom.

In a few hours, we begin three consecutive weeks of chemotherapy. This is brutal; only our faith, your faithful prayers, and thoughts of healing can sustain us. These treatments wipe us out, especially her; I am just her companion in this journey.

Natalia was in great spirits this week. We spent a lot of time laughing, dancing in bed, cuddling, eating junk food, doing our nails and putting on make-up.

This week, Natalia also discovered motorized carts at Target and Costco, and she was not only driving them without a "license" but was also driving me crazy, going up and down the aisles as I was trying to catch up with her.

"I am not a spring chicken anymore."

We shopped for headscarves, accessories and even makeup before her *Quinceañera*.

"I guess some rules can be broken sometimes."

I wore make-up for the first time when I became of age during my *Quinceañera's* rite of passage, and I was hoping to keep the same tradition with Natalia.

We are closer than ever. Lately, she has taught

me to listen to her with the ears of my heart. So often, I used to impose my will and thoughts on her, but this is changing. We are entering a mature dialogue of her likes and dislikes that never happened before, or perhaps I had never noticed or listened.

In these past twenty-nine days, she has matured so much. I look into her deep green eyes, and see a brave, poised and centered young lady even in times of adversity. She seems ready to embrace life with its perfections and imperfections. Though her physical appearance is changing fast, too fast, her beauty remains intact. It is indeed an honor to be in her presence.

Te amo,
Mommy Egli

CHAPTER 8
SUNSHINE ON THE BATTLEFIELD

Finally, brothers and sisters, whatever is true, whatever is noble, whatever is right, whatever is pure, whatever is lovely, whatever is admirable--if anything is excellent or praiseworthy--think about such things.
    - **Philippians 4:8**

Keep your face to the sun, and you will never see the shadows.
    - **Helen Keller**

May 14, 2008, 10:13 p.m.
Day 31 on our road to recovery

Dear Soldiers,

We are officially in combat. Please keep those prayers, positive thoughts of love and healing coming our way. We need them more than ever. In times when we can't pray for ourselves, we rely on you, our faithful companions. You are our strength in times of weakness and in you, we find God's grace.

On a day like today, thirty days ago, Natalia was diagnosed with cancer. Chemotherapy was started in the following week and our lives will never be the same. I write these lines with the hope of coming to terms with our new reality.

We have come so far since then and I give praise to our God Almighty for being with us every step of the way. Your constant support, love, generosity and friendship strengthen us to keep on during times of adversity.

As you already know, Natalia will be on chemo for the next three weeks. We are on day two of cycle two. This week her chemo consists of a high dose of Methotrexate with Leucovorin rescue. I know this sounds complicated, we were told that the Methotrexate is to kill all the bad cells growing in her body and the Leucovorin cleanses her system to get all the toxins out. She is responding very well to this treatment. The side effects continue to be brutal, but she remains in great spirits and strong for the most part. She is not eating much, but my mom always gets her to eat. Today, she was 109.4 pounds. This week, she is craving things that she is not allowed to have, and it breaks my heart to deny her food, but it is for her well-being.

In the midst of all we are going through, we find reasons to be thankful and things to laugh about, including ourselves. Our days begin very early in the morning and end late at night, and sometimes the day does not end at all. I have had to learn to change her IVs, keep track of medications, measure the pH level (acidity) in her body and so much more, but the most important lesson I have learned this month is that life is fragile. In a matter of seconds, our lives were turned upside down and we are trying to find our way out. Only one thing remains intact, our souls, our spirits and our faith in God. God is here with us fighting this battle.

Each day, as chaotic as it may be, I find time to be attentive to my breath. In the motion of my breath, I connect to self and ultimately to the God that lives within me. Today, Natalia covered her head with the blanket and invited me into her teepee. I sprayed her hospital linen with a lavender mist. Shortly after, she fell asleep as soft spiritual music was playing in the background and I found myself breathing her breath again. In that moment of stillness all was well and it calmed my pounding and heavy heart.

As a mother, I wish we could switch places and I can take away her pain. I feel helpless at times. It breaks my heart when she tells me, "Don't let them do this to me, mommy."

After all, she is only twelve. She is just a baby, my baby. I don't understand why these innocent creatures get cancer.

Yesterday morning on our way to the hospital, she said to me, "I want to be normal, I should be going to school." She started to call her school as

I drove to speak to her teacher, Ms. Eunice, and classmates but realized it was too early and they were not there yet. The only words that came to mind were, "This too shall pass," you will soon be back to school with your loving teachers and friends.

Many blessings,
Mommy Egli

May 16, 2008, 7:32 a.m.
Day 33 on our road to recovery

Dear Soldiers,

Thanks for fighting this battle with us. We are still in combat and will be for a while. As the *comandante* in chief, it is my duty and honor to let you know that you are fighting a good fight with us. Thanks for staying vigilant and armed with our number one weapon: prayers of love and healing.

I am so happy to inform you that Natalia has passed every test this week with flying colors. We were released early from the hospital yesterday, at 5:00 p.m., and today Friday, we only have to go in for a few hours in the early afternoon to do an MRI of Natalia's brain. She has been feeling a tingling, numbing sensation on her cheeks, hands, and feet and the neurologist wants to check it out before we begin another cycle of the same chemo she received this week.

As I mentioned before, Methotrexate is an extremely toxic type of chemo that can cause severe damage to the kidneys if not released. Thank God she responded well with the Leucovorin and was able to get rid of most of it. When we checked yesterday afternoon, she only had 56 milligrams of it in her body in comparison to the 5,000 milligrams that she had when we first started on Monday. On Wednesday, she had an MRI of the affected leg, but the results are still pending. The purpose of this MRI is to see how much of the tumor has shrunk and how many cells have been killed. Please keep in mind that even if the tumor has shrunk, the femur is severely damaged, and it will be replaced by a titanium prosthesis on the last Thursday of

July when we finish these nine weeks of chemo.

The surgery will be followed by immediate, intense physical therapy to teach her how to walk again and nineteen weeks of more chemo to prevent any future outbreaks of cancerous cells and kill any silent enemies that remain in the body.

We have a long journey ahead of us, but above all, we, remain confident that the tumor will go away. I asked her why you named the leg with the tumor Will and she confidently responded because it will go away, so at that moment I decided to call the other leg Grace. Now when we are going up and down the steps, we refer to the legs as Will and Grace, like one of my favorite shows but also because it is by the grace of God that this too shall pass, and we will continue to walk firmly in His grace.

For now, please keep praying for us. I must go now; Natalia is calling for me to assist her.

With much love and gratitude,
Mommy Egli

P.S. As soon as we left the hospital yesterday, Natalia enjoyed a large raspberry sorbet with gummy bears on top. She had been craving it since Monday and finally got it. She also had pasta with shrimp and a homemade Alfredo sauce that my sister, Jenny made her. She was 110.4 pounds yesterday and with great vital signs. Praise God!

May 18, 2008, 10:26 p.m.
Day 35 on our road to recovery

Dear Soldiers,

We have a long and challenging week ahead of us on the battlefield. We are fighting again, against Methotrexate (chemo). Remember to stay armed with our number one weapon: faithful prayers of love and healing.

Natalia had a restful weekend, and with much effort, we went to church this morning. She had the brain MRI done on Friday afternoon and was pretty upset about being poked again for the IV. The results are still pending.

The leg MRI results are back and do not show significant changes yet; they will be able to determine the number of dead cells once they take out the tumor at the end of July.

Tomorrow, Monday, we will begin our second consecutive week of chemo for cycle three. Natalia's physical appearance is changing drastically. She started losing her hair after the first cycle and last Friday, May 9th she asked my sister Jenny to finish shaving her head as India Arie's song played in the background, "I am not my hair, I am not my skin, I am the soul that lives in me." We sang along.

Natalia's courage continues to amaze me. She is embracing every moment of her condition with ease or maybe innocence. She is not resisting her reality. Thanks for visiting, for your continuous love, prayers, and encouragement.

Oh, I forgot to tell you that after Friday's MRI, Natalia was craving Mexican food and we went to a Mexican restaurant near the hospital. When Jenny and I walked in with Natalia on a wheelchair, she felt very self-conscious after some children stared at her. She said they looked frightened by her bald head. She doesn't want to wear a wig and feels very comfortable in her own skin until moments like this. It occurred to me that the only way I could convince her of the opposite was to match her new look somewhat.

After our lovely dinner, we passed a Super Cuts Hair Salon on our way to the parking lot, and we had a good laugh as I cut off all of my hair to match my girl. To me, this is just another simple way of walking this journey with her, but it will never compare to her own journey.

Con fe y esperanza,
Egli

Egli shaves her hair off in solidarity with Natalia

May 21, 2008, 9:25 p.m.
Day 38 on our road to recovery

Dear All,

Thank you very much for your words of encouragement, thoughts, prayers, love and all the wonderful things you are all doing to support us.

We had a long day today, but before I hit the sack tonight, I need to connect with you. I am delighted to inform you that Natalia has responded very well to this cycle of chemo and they are considering discharging us a day earlier without an IV. Hooray! Natalia has been coming home every night with an IV for hydration and she is also drinking, eating a bit and keeping it down. GOD IS SO GOOD!

More than ever, I believe in the power of God's healing and answered prayers. I thank you all for your faithful prayers because we feel God's presence very much at work in our lives.

We are looking forward to a restful weekend to return to the battlefield on Tuesday, strengthened and well-armed to keep fighting our battle.

Thanks for fighting a good fight with us. I hope you will never have to know about this firsthand. Natalia will soon begin cycle four of chemo which consists of Cisplatin, Doxorubicin, and Dexrazoxane.

Let us go to war, prayer warriors. Let us continue to pray faithfully and believe in our hearts that Natalia will be healed and that she will overcome this next battle too. I will try to get a few hours of sleep now, as Nurse Jenny, my sister, is on duty until midnight when medications are due.

They are having a good time watching silly shows and eating brownies with milk, while I am here sharing our day/week with you. Again, thank you very much for being part of this circle and walking this journey with us. May your hearts be peaceful and still.

With profound love and gratitude,
Mommy Egli

P.S. On our way home from the hospital tonight, Natalia decided to stop at her favorite pizzeria in Brooklyn Heights and had an entire small pie of pepperoni pizza and a medium mango sorbet. This was her first solid meal in a week. She ate every crumb in the box and loved it. She was generous enough to give Mami and me a slice to share. It is not the healthiest choice of food, but under these circumstances and after how careful I have been with our nutrition, I am not a bit concerned.

May 26, 2008, 10:28 p.m.
Day 43 on our road to recovery

Dear Soldiers,

After a restful weekend, we go back to the battlefield tomorrow. Natalia begins her fourth cycle of chemo, the last of these three consecutive cycles. Thanks for fighting a good fight with us.

This cycle of chemo will last until Saturday, and it will consist of Cisplatin, Doxorubicin, and Dexrazoxane. This combination is extremely toxic (as all) and familiar to us because it was the first cycle she had and it wiped her out.

Let us pray that this treatment continues to destroy all cancerous cells invading Natalia's body and robbing her of her health and childhood. I have a lot of mixed feelings about how toxic chemotherapy can be, but time is of the essence in our case. We have taken to natural medicine most of Natalia's life, and I am concerned about all the side effects and repercussions that all this chemo can have on her, but I don't have any other options. We need to stop this cancer from spreading and the care team says we need an aggressive and faster approach. I would prefer a natural approach, but I have been advised that if I go that route, the chances of controlling the situation are zero. This is my daughter, my one and only daughter, the only fruit of my womb. I need to trust that this approach that we have been advised to take will work. At home, I continue to give her herbal remedies and organic food. Trust and faith are all I have.

Over the weekend she developed some mouth sores and was very lethargic. My heart feels heavy tonight. My mind is telling me not to worry, but my heart aches for all that Natalia has endured and for all she will have to endure. These are the moments when I turn to you God and ask Him to hold us through these hard times. I can't see the step ahead, but I surrender my soul and daughter to You, God. I trust that You will heal her and give her the strength to make it to the finish line.

She has been so weak this weekend; she did not get out of the house since we came home from the hospital on Thursday. We cuddled a lot and looked at pictures from when she was a baby. She often said she wished she was still a baby. I had to remind her that she is back to being a baby; "Mommy has to bathe you, dress you and sometimes carry you in her arms." In my eyes, she will always be my baby.

Also, I am amazed again at my physical and emotional strength this past month. I am enduring the unimaginable and writing these lines helps me process it and makes me believe it. It is the God in me that is sustaining me and giving me the strength to overcome the supernatural.

The family gathered tonight to play bingo and to try to distract Natalia a bit, but at times, she seemed weary and distant. There was unspoken fear and worry in the room. I can sense all of our tension in expectation of what this new cycle will bring. We now know what to expect. She now knows what to expect, and all we can do is trust in God. I have nothing else to hold on to and cannot give in to despair at this time.

Her appetite was good considering the sores in her mouth, but she did not eat as much. Today, she craved lobster tails and we got her two. I picked the freshest and biggest ones from the fish market on Church Avenue. This was my goal today and every day, to cater to my girl and to keep things simple by only dealing with the step in front of me. This is all I can handle, the present moment. I steamed them, spread a little bit of melted butter, peeled some *platanos* to fry some *tostones* and she ate them all. She even asked for some more, but by the time I got back to the kitchen, she told me not to make anymore.

Again, thanks for walking this journey with us, for your supportive messages, prayers, kindness, and generosity.

I am sorry for not returning phone calls, individual emails or sending thank you notes for gifts received, but at this time things are too hectic around here. Please know that all you do for us is greatly appreciated.

With much affection and gratitude,
Mommy Egli

May 27, 2008, 8:05 a.m.
Day 44 on our road to recovery

Dear Soldiers,

I am writing to you from the hospital's waiting room; we were here at 6:00 a.m. Natalia was just seen by her team, and we have been sent home. Natalia's mouth is too sore for another cycle of chemo treatments this week.

Out of all days, I did not drive today and we are now waiting for Papi to pick us up. I sent him back to Brooklyn after he dropped us off. He gets too impatient and sad, seeing so many kids and babies fighting to live.

We will resume next Monday, June 2nd. Her blood count was normal, as well as her weight. The nurses congratulated me for taking such good care of her.

"This is my duty, and I do it with delight," I replied.

Today, she is 106.5 pounds. She needs to continue drinking and eating, and that is not a problem for Mami and me. We are Natalia's personal chefs.

Peace,
Mommy Egli

June 2, 2008, 1:27 a.m.
Day 50 on our road to recovery

Dear Companions on our Journey,
 Thank you very much for praying for Natalia's mouth sores to go away this past week, they are all gone. I thank God for His healing presence in our lives. I used all kinds of home remedies and over the counter medication to treat them and I am glad they worked. Natalia looked like a little chipmunk with puffy cheeks. It broke my heart to see her eat or even talk with her mouth full of sores. I was told that this is one of the most uncomfortable side effects of chemotherapy, one of the many downfalls, but we are going to keep pushing through. We are keeping our eyes fixed on healthier days, and we know we are going to get there.
 It is 3:00 a.m. now and Natalia is just making her way to bed. Just a month ago, this was not acceptable. She had to be in bed by 9:00 p.m., but all of our routines have been thrown off. I am not as rigid anymore and I don't sweat the little things. I can't believe I used to get so frantic when we were running a few minutes late on bedtime or when our routine was thrown off or when she did not eat healthy snacks. This is our new normal; sometimes she sleeps for almost two days straight, so I am not stressing having her awake at three in the morning.
 She was eating popcorn and watching an action movie with titi Jenny as if her life did not have enough action. She told me she will make up for her sleep while she is getting chemo tomorrow, or better, in a few hours. We have to leave for the hospital at 5:00 a.m. I hope she is as joyful as she is now when I have to wake her up in a few hours.

In the meantime, I am enjoying my 5'10" super-tall twelve-year-old bundle of joy right next to me. Natalia is in great spirits and she just told me to tell you all that she is feeling great. She is now listening to music on her new iPod to help her have sweeter dreams.

Again, thank you very much for your words of encouragement. Our faith and your prayers are getting us through these difficult days. Please keep writing to us. We have a very challenging week ahead. Natalia will be getting three different kinds of chemo at the same time, and the side effects don't wait long to kick in. We once again surrender our lives into Your hands, oh Lord.

With gratitude and affection,
Mommy Egli

June 2, 2008, 6:49 a.m.
Day 50 on our road to recovery

Hey Everyone,

    This is Natalia writing to you for a change. It is day forty-nine on our journey. We have been at the hospital for about an hour and half. We are in the Pediatric Clinic waiting for a room on the ninth floor at Memorial Sloan Kettering.

    I am in good spirits and feeling strong. I will need every ounce of strength to get through this week. The mouth sores healed as mommy gave me a lot of yucky remedies and I had no choice but to take them. I also ate a lot of yummy stuff. My family takes excellent care of me and they are continually feeding me, and asking me what I want. They were always attentive to me before, but now that I am sick, they care for me even more.

    I am waiting for the Osteosarcoma team to call me in so we can get this party started. I just finished getting my finger stuck. This is the routine every time I come. It hurts sometimes, but unfortunately, I am getting used to it since I get stuck almost every day.

    I am using the computer in the waiting room and just catching up on my mom's entries. I just read what she wrote at 3:00 a.m. when I was wired up watching a movie and listening to some music.

    I kept her up late after she wrote that journal entry. I had her play a game of cards. Mommy hates playing any games. She actually can't play any, but she tries. I just could not go to sleep last night. I was actually watching a horror movie hence, why I could not go to sleep. It was terrific; "Untraceable" was exactly what I needed to watch to distract me a little bit.

Ok, it is now time to get this party started. I will write again when I bounce back. In the meantime, I send you some peace, love and strength.

Natalia, xoxo kisses

June 3, 2008, 11:45 p.m.
Day 51 on our road to recovery

Dear Companions on our Journey,

    I am just writing to you briefly to let you know how difficult the past forty-eight hours have been for us. I don't even know when one day ends and the other one begins anymore. I just realized it is past midnight and we are still going strong. Today was another dark day for us, but not as dark as yesterday. We experienced some sunshine today when Natalia woke up for a little while and asked for ice cream.

    The side effects seem to get more brutal as we move along in the process, or maybe she is getting weaker. We are on the third day of cycle four, and the side effects have been so strong that Natalia has been sedated most of the time. We had to carry her out of the hospital in our arms like when she was a baby. I don't understand why they don't let us stay overnight, or hospitalize us for the week. We have to be back here at the crack of dawn, and she doesn't realize when we bring her home from the hospital at night or when we bring her back in the morning. Discharging the children home every night is the hospital's protocol and a way of keeping some normalcy in the child's life, but most the of time Natalia is disoriented and unaware of her comings and goings.

    I put on and take off her coat in bed each day. I carry her to put her on the wheelchair to the car, lay her in the back seat and let her lean her head on Mami's lap while I drive. She seems unconscious throughout the whole process and her eyes never open. Sometimes I am afraid to look at the rear view mirror because it looks as if Mami was holding a corpse. I can't even contemplate that thought. I try to keep my eyes fixed on the road and stay focused on better days ahead. I bring her home with an IV backpack which usually stays with me in the front seat.

Today, after sleeping for over thirty-eight hours, she opened her eyes when titi Aissa came to visit. The first thing she asked for was ice cream. Hearing her voice again was like music to my ears. It is great to see her awake; she asked us to take her for ice cream and pizza. We took her downstairs to the hospital's cafeteria in her wheelchair. As titi Aissa was pushing her, she was rolling her IV pole. Natalia was determined to get her ice cream.

Once we got to the first floor and saw the bright sun shining outside, we took her out to the sidewalk instead. They both sat under a tree outside the hospital while I went across the street to get the lemon coolata she was craving, not ice cream anymore. The sun shone especially for me today. I looked up at the sky while I waited for the light to change to cross the street. I got a glimpse of heaven when I saw my precious Natalia awake asking for lemon coolatta, ice cream from Baskin Robbins and pepperoni pizza. She is very specific with her cravings these days, and I do my best to get them right away because I never know when she is going to be awake again.

She was only awake for thirty-six minutes today, and it was delightful.

Stepping out of the hospital walls for fresh air and letting the sunshine warm up our souls was refreshing. What a treat! Thank You, God, for these little blessings. I don't take them for granted. Thank You for reassuring me that my girl is somewhere in there and that she is going to wake up soon. Thank You for letting me hear her voice again today. Thank You for letting me look into her green eyes. Thank You for her cravings and for my adventurous friend to share this moment with me. These were the best thirty-six minutes of my life.

Seeing her awake, alert, eating, drinking, and enjoying a few moments of peace in the sunshine was like being in paradise. This brief moment of alertness gave me the strength to get me through the rest of the day. I have been freaking out seeing her sleep for days. When I ask her team, they insist that it is too debilitating for her to stay awake, nauseous.

I have been lying next to her, caressing her cheeks, pleading with God, laying my hands over her and praying for a miracle. I am constantly putting my hand on her chest, checking if her heart is still beating and putting my fingers under her nostrils to make sure she is breathing. This is what I used to do when she was an infant. Her heartbeat is my most comforting melody. I curl up in bed with her, keep my hand on her chest and fall asleep next to her until a nurse comes to check on her, or the aid comes to check the temperature, or the maintenance guy comes to sweep for the fifth time as if we were building toys or throwing up confetti in the "2x2" hospital room. More and more, I realize that life is so brief, life is just a brief breath. *La vida es solo un suspiro.*

Tomorrow is a big day. While many schools are preparing for graduations and having their proms, the hospital is having a prom for all the pediatric patients, those graduating and those who will not live to go to their prom or graduation. Everyone is talking about this grand event; I hear they transform part of the cafeteria into a ballroom. I know my daughter will love to go to her own prom and many other celebrations, but we will get all dolled up and be part of the festivities for practice sake. All patients, including infants and their families were given gowns donated by designers to attend this special event. I was given a dress too, but I could not fit into it, not even with my mom's girdle on. I have put on some weight sitting in a hospital room every day. Sometimes I walk around this floor a couple of times a week, but I often get discouraged whenever I see patients in worse condition than my daughter's or when I hear stories that do not have happy endings.

I need to stay focused. Our story is not the same as others and will have a happy ending. I will wear one of my mom's dresses for the prom. Natalia, my sister, and mom, were given gorgeous gowns. I hope today is better and that we can make it to the party. It means a lot to me to share a dance with my daughter like old times, even if I now have to spin her in a wheelchair.

Before chemo started on Monday morning, Natalia was interviewed by Charles Gibson from ABC News about the prom and her condition; she even showed him her leg. She was also taped trying on her gown attached to a chemo IV and they will tape us again tomorrow at the party if she is able to get out of bed. They even got me on camera when I finally found a dress to fit me.

And where is God in all of this? God is right here and right now. We are counting our blessings in the midst of this tragedy.

So many people and organizations have come together to give us a few moments of joy at this hospital prom. God is in the generosity of all the benefactors, the designers who donated dresses, accessories, shoes, bags, food and entertainment for us to celebrate. God is in the music, the small details in turning a boring hospital cafeteria into a ballroom. God is here with us. God is in my mother's strength and my sister's silliness. God is in Natalia's thirty-six minutes of alertness asking for ice cream, pizza, and lemonade. God is in the refuge that I find when I write to you and the support of your companionship.

With much love and hope,
Mommy Egli - Proud mother of the bravest girl I know, Natalia.

June 4, 2008, 6:36 a.m.
Day 52 on our road to recovery

Dear Companions on our journey,

    A new day has just begun and we are now at the hospital waiting for Natalia's care team to arrive. As usual, we are expected to be here until the early evening, but I am delighted to inform you that with much effort and determination, my princess was able to make it to the hospital's prom yesterday. In my eyes, she looked stunning. I believe the segment will air on today's World Nightly News with Charles Gibson on Channel 7. I forgot to ask what time it will air. This was another brutal week for Natalia, but they wanted to follow her around and document her journey. I don't know how much will be aired tonight, but hearing her explain her condition so thoroughly and with so much courage, strengthens me. Hopefully, they were able to capture how intense this week has been and how brave Natalia is. She indeed has the heart of a warrior.

    I have to admit that it was difficult to be in a festive atmosphere and get all dolled up under these circumstances, but it was a nice distraction. Although Natalia was not feeling well, my baby looked regal. We love to party and dance together, and this situation does not change that.

    It was difficult and emotional to see her in a wheelchair on the dance floor as we took turns with her. She was too weak and groggy to stand up the entire time. Mami, Jenny, and I, along with very dear friends Aissa, Sandy and Veronica surrounded her and spun her while we each took turns spinning her IV pole. It was like a movie scene. We cried tears of joy, fear and hope as we danced, rejoiced and made the best of the situation.

She surprised us all when she heard the Cha Cha slide, one of her favorite line dances. She asked for her crutches and attempted to dance on one leg. About fifty kids were celebrating with their families. Some of them with cancer that is in remission; some are missing a leg, an arm, an eye, but most of them are undergoing treatment and have no hair like Natalia. All are full of life, dancing and screaming with joy on the dance floor, while the rest of the outside world is sweating the little stuff, rushing and complaining. Life is so ironic.

With much love and *esperanza*,
Mommy Egli - Proud mom of a princess with an untamable spirit and very happy feet.

P.S. When we left the hospital last night, she asked me to take her to Red Lobster for dinner. She ate half asleep, connected to an IV, but she kept her dinner in. I don't know when she will wake up again.

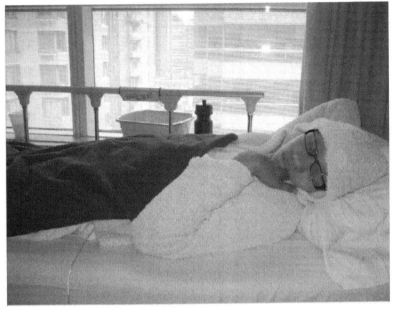

Natalia, during one of the chemotherapy rounds.

June 6, 2008, 9:50 a.m.
Day 54 on our road to recovery

My Dearest Companions,

We are home today and I am giving Natalia my undivided attention.

She just woke up and wants breakfast. I am running to get it ready. It is a good day around here. I am counting my blessings. It is the little things that matter.

Much love,
Mommy Egli

I am the happiest mom in the universe. It feels great to have my baby home!

June 9, 2008, 7:26 a.m.
Day 57 on our road to recovery

My Dear Faithful Companions,

I would like to start this Monday morning by giving thanks to our Creator for the air we breathe, for keeping us alive, for blessing us with all we need and for the gift of family, friends, caregivers and so much more.

Natalia is still asleep and before my day gets hectic, I want to share a bit about our great and hot weekend. Oops, Natalia just woke up, got to go!

I am back... 5:04 p.m.

Natalia spent most of the weekend in bed, but on Saturday afternoon, we went to a bingo fundraiser event put together by my amazing circle of friends, The Vermont sisters. We are all New Yorkers, but for over twenty years, we have been going on an annual retreat put together by us in Weston, Vermont. This bingo event was held at Natalia's school, The Young Women's Leadership Academy, with the intention to help us out. It was awesome! I am humbled by the outpour of love, support and solidarity.

I am convinced that love is the highest force that keeps us going and this past Saturday, we were strengthened by the power of love, the gift of friendship and The Vermont Sisters' generosity. If you ask me again, where is God in all of this? I would tell you, God is there. God is in the compassion and solidarity others are showing towards us, the unmerited favors received.

The bingo event was our first gathering since our lives were changed 56 days ago and it was great to see so many smiling faces, and to be hugged. Natalia's life has touched so many lives.

Again, to my Vermont sisters and to all those who attended and contributed, gracias! May all the good you do return to you double-fold. I am overwhelmed by your thoughtfulness and faith in action. I have realized I am not carrying this burden alone. Thanks for making it lighter for me to bear. Natalia is still overwhelmed with how much she is loved and all the people praying for us.

Natalia is having a good day; we went to her amusement park this morning, Costco. She put into her motorized scooter all the things she wants Mami to cook for her this week, lobster tails, shrimp, crab legs and some other yummy stuff. We were always seafood lovers, but lately, all she wants to eat is seafood, paella, New England clam chowder, shrimp scampi and more lobster tails. I am going to have to marry a fisherman to keep up with her cravings.

Well, as long as she eats, she can continue asking for seafood. Sometimes she goes two to three days without eating, but when she eats, she makes up for it. I am not complaining.

Until later, my friends, I have got to get dinner ready.

Mommy Egli,
Proud mommy of a princess who loves seafood so much that she may turn into a little mermaid soon.

June 11, 2008, 7:52 a.m.
Day 59 on our road to recovery

Dear Faithful Companions,

Thank you very much for praying all infections away so far. It is mid-week and Natalia is still infection free. This is a very risky week because after last week's treatments, white blood cells, the ones that fight infections are expected to drop.

Natalia is still asleep; I just want to share with you yesterday's doctor's visit. She continues to be infection free, her hemoglobin level is normal at 11.6 (no need for transfusions yet), white blood cells count at 1.6, not the highest but stable and she weighs 103.7 pounds. She dropped about six pounds, but she is not connected to an IV this week, so I think most of those six pounds were retention of fluids from last week.

Yesterday, when we came out of the doctor's office, I was approached by the mother of a nine-year-old girl who is also a cancer patient at the hospital.

She said to me, "What are you doing to keep your daughter so well? We are only one week ahead of you in the treatments, and my daughter has had four hospitalizations with infections, transfusions, and complications. Your daughter is responding so well to the treatments and always looks so strong and happy regardless of her circumstances. What are you giving her? I envy you!"

I was shocked by her words. My eyes opened up wide, and I quickly said, "Prayers, lots of prayers, and lots of faithful companions praying for us and walking this journey with us."

So, for this, and for so much more, I thank you

all. I also ask that you pray for this nine-year-old girl suffering so much, as well as all the other cancer patients on our pediatric floor surrounding us. They need to be surrounded by constant prayers and courage to keep on going.

For those who missed yesterday's ABC News broadcast on the pediatric prom at Sloan Kettering, you can watch it online. Go to abcnews.com and then to WorldNews.

Yesterday, Natalia and I visited what will be our new home in Harlem in August. We have been waiting for this construction to be finished for the past two years. Hooray! We blessed our future home. Our friend, Rev. Walter, prepared a beautiful prayer service and prayed for God to abide in every room, and for us to live a long, healthy and happy lives in it.

We had lots of fun discussing some decorating ideas with our friends, Sandy, Veronica, Mami, Jenny, Aissa and Walter. This was supposed to be a quick inspection of the condo before closing. Management had no idea it was going to turn into a two-hour ceremonial event.

After we inspected the condo, I informed the management office that I wanted to be left alone with my friends so that I could dedicate this condo to my Creator and Provider before we move in. This is our new sanctuary, and we want Jesus to be the center of it. I gave Natalia the key to the condo; this is my gift to her. It has been my heart's deepest desire since I left the house I had with her dad to be a homeowner again. By the grace of God, this dream has been accomplished. Thank you, God, for exceeding my expectations. Our condo is more than what we could have dreamed of. For this, and so much more, we are eternally grateful.

I was like a kid in a toy store running around in our soon to be new home. The closets are enormous; we have lots of them, double closets with double doors and even four doors in one of them. I was going in and out of them. Sandy cracked up when she found me submerged in the tub in my master bathroom, fully dressed and feet up. She caught me talking to myself, pretending as though I was having a bubble bath in an empty tub. Thank You, God, in the midst of the storm, You give me a little rainbow to keep me hopeful.

Thank You, God, for showing me every day that our dreams don't have an expiration date and that we can trust You with our lives. Thank You for confirming that You pay attention even to the most intimate details of our lives. I love You beyond words because You first loved me.

With much love, faith and hope,
Mommy Egli - Proud mom of the bravest girl I know and a new homeowner in the midst of chaos.

June 14, 2008, 10:09 a.m.
Day 62 on our road to recovery

My Dearest Faithful *Compañeros y Compañeras en la Batalla*,

Our God is a good God, a merciful and loving God. A God that makes the impossible possible. He is a faithful God that is walking by our side or better yet, carrying us through our journeys when we tremble and can't even walk for ourselves.

Today is a month and two days of this agony on our road to recovery. Healing and restoration are already happening. Yesterday, we took Natalia for her second checkup this week, and she is doing great. This is music to my ears. I just want to praise You and give You thanks. Gracias mi Dios, thank you and thank you all for your continued prayers.

Paulette, the Osteosarcoma team's nurse practitioner could not believe the results of Natalia's lab tests. She had to look at them three times and even checked Natalia's chart to make sure that the chemo had been given to her last week. I had to reassure her that I had seen every drop of chemo drop from the IV enter her veins. I prayed that each drop kills the bad cells, and heal her body.

She told me, "Keep doing whatever it is you are doing."

"We are praying, trusting and believing that God will deliver us," I replied.

"This is too good to be true, but it is true. Your daughter is responding very well. I thought I had a different chart, but these are her results. Prayers are powerful, keep praying my friend and get out of here quick," she responded, smiling. "Hurry! Go!"

I was so excited that I started to jump and dance with joy in the examining room, while translating in Spanish to my mom what Paulette had said and asking her to push the wheelchair faster so, we could get out of the hospital quicker. We spent the rest of the day at my brother's backyard. It was beginning to feel like summer. Natalia was playing for the first time with her cousin Kimberly, and other friends while the grown-ups were catching up. It was amazing to see how her peers were accommodating her to play with them.

They all know to not break Will, so they all took turns pushing her in the wheelchair and making sure her crutches were nearby in case she wanted to get up. She was not connected to an IV backpack this week; she was drinking and eating on her own, laughing, and keeping a positive attitude as always.

Last week we were warned that Natalia's hemoglobin was going to drop this week and that she was going to need a blood transfusion. If you were to see her now, you would not think this was the same kid under treatment last week and with this prognosis. We were also told that there was a greater chance for hospitalization this week due to a possible drop of white blood cells, needed to fight infections.

She is infection free and all the numbers are high.

Thank You God, I can only praise You and give You thanks. With Your presence in our lives, we can walk on fire and not get burned. Your shield and protection are greater than anything. We keep on surrendering and holding on to You. Thanks for Your refuge and warm embrace, we know that it is by Your grace that we have come this far and for this and so much more I sing Your name and give You thanks and praise.

Thank You God, for changing the forecast. You have turned the expected storm into a beautiful clear sunny day and week. Natalia has been eating everything in sight. Her latest cravings are steamed crab legs, grilled lobster tails, *tostones*, rice and beans, *mofongo con chicharrones*. Expensive taste, right? She seems to be thirstier than usual and drinking a lot of homemade, cranberry and grapefruit juices. We are all at her service, anything she craves and at whatever time we make sure we get it for her.

It has truly been a great week. So much so that just an hour away from my student's graduation at Cristo Rey New York High School, Natalia told me. "I know how important it is for you to see your students graduate. This is the school's first graduation, and you have worked very hard there, mommy.

"Let's get me ready; we are going!"

It was pure madness to get her ready and get to Harlem before they walked out. I had to give her all her medications for her to be comfortable during the ceremony. Getting the car was crazy - there was major construction happening on the street we parked, but we managed to get it out. It was a typical New York City day with sirens from ambulances and police filling the air, but we were determined to make it.

We had no time to waste. Natalia and Mami were waiting for me in front of our building with the wheelchair, crutches and everything else that I now have to carry for her comfort. I guess the authorities saw in my face, a determined teacher/mother on a mission, eager to get to my students' graduation. They stopped the traffic and allowed me to get my SUV through a back street because I was ready to get on the sidewalk to get the car out of there.

I am crazy about my students and when I had to leave them to have surgery just before Natalia was diagnosed, I promised them I was going to be back to see them graduate. I had no idea Natalia was going to get sick and how hard it was going to be to fulfill that promise, but God always makes a way.

When I got to my school, the students were ready to walk down the aisle and they greeted me with the warmth I needed. One of the lions, as we called our students, shouted to the crowd, "You see, she kept her promise, she made it!" To my surprise, the school had rented a cap and gown for me to walk down the aisle with them on their first graduation.

It meant the world to my students that I share this experience with them. Natalia and Mami were surprised to see me walk into St. Cecilia's Church with the rest of the faculty. They smiled from ear to ear and gave me the thumbs up. I was elated. It was such a surreal moment to be able to escape from my new reality and join my colleagues and students in celebrating their victory.

Having my daughter infection free this week and seeing my lions graduate were the highlights of my week. Thank You God for Your everlasting grace.

We are expected to go back to the hospital for Cycle Five on Monday, June 23rd. In the meantime, let us stay together in faithful prayers. There are so many other things and issues going on right now that can rob me of this joy, but I refuse to be sucked into negativity. We are keeping a drama free environment, a positive atmosphere and an attitude of gratitude. Maintaining this attitude is a top priority in Natalia's care plan. I invite you to do the same. Remove from your environment anything that is toxic which does not serve you. They are like cancer and we are under treatment.

With much love and gratitude,
Mommy Egli - Natalia's happy mom and
Cristo Rey New York High School proud teacher.

CHAPTER 9
PERFECTION IN THE IMPERFECTION

Being confident of this, that he who began a good work in you will carry it on to completion until the day of Christ Jesus.
   - Philippians 1:6

I always find beauty in things that are odd and imperfect - they are much more interesting.
   - Marc Jacobs

June 19, 2008, 5:55 a.m.
Day 67 on our road to recovery

Dear Companions,

We are having a great week, Natalia is in great spirits and this makes every minute of every hour amazing. She is eating well and dancing to her own beat on her crutches at all kinds of odd hours. She has been drawing and painting with the brightest colors she can find on her palette.

Keeping our eyes fixed on the prize keeps us sane. Today, we are a day closer to a full recovery. This morning we are getting ready to go to the hospital for CAT scans and bone MRIs. They want to make sure that the tumor is shrinking and that the cancer has not metastasized or affected other organs. This coming Monday, we begin chemo again for two consecutive weeks. Natalia postponed her surgery initially scheduled for July 17th to July 24th a week after her 13th birthday. It seems like she is calling the shots at the hospital.

"You are not operating on me a day before my thirteenth birthday," were her exact words to her orthopedic surgeon.

She also told her that she was planning a birthday party with my sister's assistance at Prospect Park and that she was welcome to join.

I stood in the examination room in awe of my daughter's maturity and autonomy over her own body. That is my child, telling her surgeon what to do. It is that joyful spirit and ownership of her own body that keeps her strong and centered in the midst of the battle.

I feel truly privileged to be Natalia's mom. She teaches me new things about life and myself every single day. Thank you for giving me a new perspective on life and for showing me the importance of celebrating even when things are not like we expect them to be.

Con mucha fe y esperanza,
Mommy Egli - A warrior's proud mom.

June 23, 2008, 10:10 p.m.
Day 71 on our road to recovery

Dear Warriors,

Today we started cycle five out of twenty cycles of chemotherapy, (Methotrexate). Blood counts were normal, as well as her weight, 108 pounds, and 1 ounce. The results from last week's tests do not show any progress. There is inflammation around the tumor, but the team said it is from the chemo. They are not able to determine how much of the tumor has shrunk, or how many cells have died, until they remove the tumor and study it on July 24th. The big operation is almost a month away, and we continue to trust in God. We believe that the God that has brought us this far is not going to leave us now. He keeps promises, and will deliver them.

Natalia was the first one to get up this morning, watching her so pensive in bed was intense. She woke up anxious in anticipation of the day ahead but did not say anything. She was hoping and praying for the chemo to be canceled due to a few mosquito bites she got at my cousin's BBQ party on Saturday, but the treatment will go on as planned.

As time passes and the side effects intensify, she is getting anxious about the start of a new cycle. She now knows what to expect and I don't blame her. Chemo side effects are no joke and the medications to suppress the side effects don't seem to help much. I see before my eyes how she has quickly transformed from a perky kid into a lethargic, sick one, and this breaks my heart.

Every time we begin a new cycle, I feel like I lose my child to unconsciousness. It is Monday, and Natalia won't be back to her full self until about Thursday or Friday. She will have no clue of what goes on, except for the frequent vomiting and physical discomfort. I feel helpless.

I can only pray and trust in God's greater plan. I can very easily become bitter and begin to blame You, God, but I refuse to go there. I trust You, not because You are God, and I was taught to honor and respect You, but because I know that You have a bigger and better plan for our lives. I know deep in my heart that this is not how the story ends. Help me to continue to stay present and surrender to Your will. You are all I got, and I continue to give myself to You, even with this yucky feeling of helplessness I feel as a mom. I continue to surrender to You.

Today, Natalia was only able to find comfort laying on me in bed and as each drop of chemo was entering her veins, I felt her absence. I felt her leaving me and then, she was deep asleep on my chest. The hardest part today was seeing her being accessed, which is when the nurse inserts a big, sharp needle into the Mediport on her chest. It is like a stab in my heart. These easy access tubes are inserted into her chest and connected to her Vena Cava - I was told that it helped to avoid the constant poking, since her veins are scarce now. This procedure is still very uncomfortable.

My niece accompanied us to the hospital today. She covered her eyes and held on to me while Natalia was being accessed.

Natalia was brave and although, she felt anxious, she told her nurse, Andrea, how to draw her blood easier and how to flush the IV through the Mediport. Again, Natalia is in charge of her body, and she knows it very well. She sees me with my medical chart questioning physicians, researching and making educated decisions as her best advocate, so I guess the apple doesn't fall far from the tree. Holding the syringe as she usually does, she told the nurse to let her flush her IV. Another lesson learned; let go and trust my child. She is brave, brilliant and in control.

I don't blame Natalia for not wanting to go back to the hospital today. As much as I did not want to go either, this process will bring her back to health. We continue to keep our eyes fixed on the final prize, which is a long healthy life, a full recovery and wellness. It is perfectly normal to feel overwhelmed and helpless, but we cannot allow our fears to paralyze us. We must stay strong, focused and keep moving forward.

I hesitated to write this tonight because I feel overwhelmed with so many mixed emotions. We are feeling tired and sad. We miss life the way it was. We miss being at the beach this summer, going on vacation, walking our puppy, Princess, going for ice cream, running, rollerblading, riding our bikes, being at the playground. She misses standing on her own two feet and being able to walk without the crutches, or just finding enjoyment even if doing nothing. We are physically, mentally and emotionally exhausted, and dear God, we come to You to be refreshed, invigorated and touched by Your Holy Spirit.

Father God, if You allow me, I need to vent for a few minutes. I miss my baby girl! We miss each other and the simplicity we had. Instead, we are learning to cope with this crisis, finding enjoyment in our reality of learning to accept things the way they are. I am learning to be the mother of a critically ill child, and this is not always easy.

I am learning to mourn my loss. She is learning how to endure, how to be sick yet, keep on going. And when she can't go on anymore, she is learning to lean on those who love her and let us carry her through these dark hours. I need Your strength more than ever because I am growing a little weary.

I know that the sun will shine for us again, I know that this too shall pass, and I trust that God will return my child to full health, but in the meantime, I need to accept my feelings, feel the void, the silence, the emptiness of our home. There's no running around, jumping, yelling, dancing or any disagreeing with me. I miss you, Natalia. All I have right now is your heartbeat, your breath next to mine and the hope you will wake up from your sedated sleep soon. Sleep my little child, one day, you will wake up, and this will all seem like a nightmare or one of mommy's
horror stories.

She is asleep now, we have a long night ahead of us which include having to wake her up every few hours to medicate her and measure the acidity or pH level in her body through her urine.

Simply Egli today

June 24, 2008, 10:27 p.m.
Day 72 on our road to recovery

Dear Faithful Companions,

Thank you for walking this journey with us. We got through the day and made it back home safely. After being curled up in the hospital bed all day, we are finally home curled up in our own bed. Every morning we hope to come home after treatment, but sometimes she is admitted. It is good to be home tonight.

It takes an army to get Natalia out of here in the mornings and an army to get her back at night. Thank God for my family and a great community of friends. We are so thankful for the portable ramp our church family got us to get the wheelchair up and down the steps at the entrance of my parents' building.

I don't even know how to judge how today went. I only know that we got through it. I get a glimpse of what Natalia is feeling and cannot even imagine what it is like to be her. Last night was a long night waking up every couple of hours for medications and to measure her pH level, but once again, we got through it by the grace of God.

Natalia was a bit confused and disoriented when she woke up this morning. She asked me to pack her backpack with all of her summer reading books as if we were packing to go away for the summer. Her Social Studies teacher, Tamara came to visit her yesterday at the hospital. She brought her some of the projects she had done during the year, along with a book and a movie. She enjoyed the visit, and it was the only time she was alert during the day. This morning she did not know if it had been a dream or if her teacher had actually visited. Every time she opened her eyes today, she would ask me, "Is my teacher here?"

My dad and niece, Dariela came with us to the hospital today, but Natalia only wanted me lying next to her, so we curled up in bed all day. She asked me to hold her tight, but not too tight, and I did. This is all that matters to me right now. I just woke her up for her medication. She has been a bit delirious this week, but when she is alert, she has difficulties keeping track of time, things and places. I don't blame her.

Just a few minutes ago she had a tantrum as I was giving her medications for the night. She was begging me not to take her back to the hospital tomorrow.

"I don't want to do this anymore mommy. I am tired of taking so much medication, don't you get it? All I have in my stomach is medicine! I can't eat, I am tired, I want to give up, I want to go back in time and not have cancer! I want it to go away!"

I wanted to react and tell her she could not give up now, but as hard as it was to see her enraged and hear what was coming out of her mouth, I stayed quiet and let her be.

This is the first time I have seen her react to this sturdy cancer. As devastating as it was to see this meltdown, I can only agree with her and wish for this to go away also. I wish magic was real. I wish that she could wake up cured tomorrow and we could let go of the twenty-something treatments left, the surgeries and everything else. But I also know the only way out, is through.

So, Father God once again, I come to You to wipe off my tears and this feeling of helplessness and a heavy heart. Give my daughter the strength to keep going on. Let the morning dawn bring us a renewed spirit and a renewed mind. I surrender into Your hands, hold us tight. Please, and never let us go. This too shall pass, although it is hard to see now.

When we got home from the hospital, I took a break and went for a run in the park while my sister and my mom took over my shift. I am not a runner, yet I ran four miles with the hopes of running away from my life, forcing myself to stay present and let go of my fears. Every step was a conscious step and breath, rejoicing in the beauty of this summer day, the gift of nature and our Creator. I focused on the beautiful trees and acres of green pasture.

I told myself, "One day my grass will get greener." I was reminded that this world is still a beautiful place. This was an opportunity to shift gears and refocus.

When I got home, Natalia was up and feeling a bit better. She asked my sister for pasta and shrimp and was able to digest it. She is deep asleep now until 2:00 a.m. when she is due for her next round of medications. Seeing her eat her dinner and keep it in was my sunshine on this dark day. A sign that things are getting better.

Thank You, God!
Egli

June 26, 2008, 11:28 p.m.
Day 74 on our road to recovery

Dear Faithful Companions,

We made it to the finish line this week. Natalia passed every test today with flying colors. We are home until Monday, resting and recharging ourselves with the strength needed to begin cycle six next week, the last cycle before the big operation on July 24th.

Natalia is still a little weak, but she is eating more and staying awake longer. Today, on our way home, she was craving sushi with a lot of wasabi and soy sauce. As soon as I got off the Brooklyn Bridge, I got some for her on Montague Street, near my Alma Mater, St. Francis College. She ate them all and could have had some more, but I am really pushing it by letting her eat raw fish. It is not recommended in her condition, but she wanted it. She even tricked my mom into eating wasabi by telling her it was guacamole. Mami was so naive that she ate the wasabi and her mouth was on fire. That is how I know Natalia's coming back to herself when she starts pulling pranks like this one.

When we got home, she took a long nap and woke up asking for pepperoni pizza and tamarind balls. Weird combination, but my Papi went out and got them for her. So far she is keeping everything down, with much effort though. She was just complaining about a belly ache. It could be from her weird food combinations or all the medications in her system.

Today, Natalia started the day making plans to go to Dorney Park and bike ride after the surgery. She is slowly gaining back her strength, but she says her joints still hurt a lot. Mid-morning, she was able to find some comfort and sleep while my Mami massaged her with lavender oil. They have such a special bond and it is adorable to see the relationship they have. The nurses walked in while she was sleeping and said that our little room smelled like a spa. Well, that is our daily intention, to mentally take ourselves to a spa to endure.

As tired as I am, I felt the need to write and share these moments with you. Believe it or not, I look forward to my journal entries. I truly feel the presence of all those far and near praying for us. I am also confident that the presence of God is here with us.

When we got home, I went for another four-mile speed walk/run while Natalia napped. As I took each step for her and me, I was consciously shaking off the fears, anxieties and frustrations that kept me down this week. I wonder if people think I am crazy when at times, I shake dance while I run. We are doing everything in our power to stay focused, positive and strong on our road to wellness and full recovery. We have no time to waste consumed in toxic thoughts, fears of the future and resentments of the past. I am letting go, all we have is this breath, this moment, and we are embracing it with courage. Quitting is not an option for us. This is what we tell ourselves, so let us continue lighting Natalia's life with love, peace, and healing energy.

Con mucha fe y esperanza,
Egli - Proud mommy of a true warrior.

July 2, 2008, 2:26 p.m.
Day 80 on our road to recovery

Hi All,

It is me, Natalia, and I am at the hospital right now. I just asked mommy to get me a slice of pizza with pepperoni on it. I don't like to eat the hospital food.

I am so excited about my birthday coming up on July 18th. It is so important to celebrate life and be thankful. It is 3:30 p.m. right now, and I leave the hospital at around 5:00 p.m. I just came in today for IV hydration as well as tomorrow. Hopefully, I won't have to come on Friday. This is the last week of chemo until the surgery after my birthday. The other days I come to the hospital are going to be for checkups and preparation for the big day. Alright TTYL. (Talk to you later for those not keeping up with the youngins).

Hugs and Kisses,
Natalia

July 3, 2008, 11:23 p.m.
Day 81 on our road to recovery

Dear Companions,

I am compelled to share the following lyrics to express how we feel at this moment. Please feel free to sing along with us:

> We've come this far by faith
> Leaning on the Lord.
> Trusting in His Holy word,
> He never failed me yet
> Oh oh oh oh…

Ok, this is all I remember from Donnie McClurkin's version of this gospel song that we often sing in our church. I just wanted to let you know how good our God is and how thankful we are for bringing us this far on our road to recovery. Natalia's care team is still amazed at her strength and resilience. With God's grace, she managed to finish six consecutive aggressive cycles of chemotherapy with no fevers, no blood transfusions and no infections. It was not easy, but it could have been worse.

We just finished cycle six today; this is our last cycle before the big surgery on July 24th. We are both in great spirits, looking forward to getting some rest and return to the hospital renewed and ready to continue the fight. Next week we'll go back for regular checkups. Sushi and pepperoni pizzas are the cravings of the week.

Eternally grateful for the love and prayers.
Estamos muy agradecidas por sus oraciones, amor y apoyo.

Con amor,
Egli - Proud mommy of a soon to be teen.

July 16, 2008, 12:29 a.m.
Day 94 on our road to recovery

Dear Faithful Companions,

By the grace of God, all is well. Natalia is counting the days until her 13th birthday which is in two days, this Friday, July 18th.

This morning during our pillow talk, she whispered in my ears that she could not wait to blow out her shimmery birthday candles. She still can't make up her mind about which cake flavor she wants. She wants strawberry cheesecake as well as a chocolate cake with Oreo cookies on top. She may get them both since the festivities will begin on Thursday and end on Sunday with a sleepover. She is truly loved by all.

She is also counting the days to her big surgery on July 24th and being able to walk again with the "new leg," as she calls it now. She is not really getting a new leg, just an internal titanium prosthesis attached from the femur to the knee. During the surgery, they are removing the tumor and affected parts of the femur to replace it with metal. They will cut high enough and low enough from the tumor to make sure the cancer does not spread, I was told. She is looking forward to retaking long walks, riding her bike and simply being back on her feet. One of our first walks will be walking across the Brooklyn Bridge.

The procedure will be long, and I am kindly asking everyone I know to continue to pray for us and keep sending positive thoughts and healing blessings. We are expected to be in the hospital for a week or two. After surgery, she will begin physical therapy the next day, and chemotherapy will resume again in two weeks. She has thirteen more cycles of chemo to go. Wow, it just hit me that she has thirteen more cycles to go and she is turning thirteen. We are not superstitious, but the coincidence in the number caught my attention.

The road ahead looks rough, but we are focusing on the battles won and the bright and smooth side of our journey. Life is great, my friends, and we are embracing every part of it with its perfections and imperfections. It gets difficult and overwhelming at times, but this too shall pass. One step at a time, one breath at a time, one day at a time.

Muchas gracias,
Egli - Very proud mom of a warrior and soon to be a teen.

July 17, 2008, 9:30 p.m.
Day 95 on our road to recovery

Dear Faithful Companions,

Along with the market crashing on Wall Street, cancer has affected and permeated every area of our lives including our finances. My lifelong savings went toward the down payment of our condo before Natalia's diagnosis and I am currently on a non-paid leave from work. Being by Natalia's side at this point is my only priority which is not an option, but I still have all the responsibilities of a household as a single parent, and I need to pay bills.

I have always been a better giver than a receiver and throughout this whole process, one of the hardest lessons has been to receive. Our tribe has been very supportive of us and before we even ask for anything, they are there with it. My Vermont sisters have had two fundraiser events. My job has also been very generous, and on Sunday, we had a flea market/fundraiser at our church. Even the firefighters showed up to support us at our church. I also took out my wedding dress from 1995 to sell it, but when Natalia saw it hanging from the awning of the church, she asked me to put it down and not to sell it. I doubt that she will wear it when she gets married, but I guess it has sentimental value to her.

I have already sold my most precious jewelry pieces that had sentimental value like the gold chain with my nameplate and a bracelet I asked Papi to buy me instead of giving me a *Quinceañera* party. I preserved these pieces because I know how hard he worked to get them for me. He had them put on Lay-Away and paid them off in small installments until my 15th birthday. After they presented the jewelry to me on my birthday in November, a few months later, I somehow convinced Mami to give me a party in the Dominican Republic with our relatives during our summer vacation. Papi could not get the time off from work, but my godfather represented him. He danced the waltz with me and did the changing of shoe ceremony that symbolizes the coming of age.

I called Cash for Gold after seeing their commercial on television, and they sent me a post-

Egli's Quinceañera in Santiago, Dominican Republic

aged bag to send in all my gold. My dad paid hundreds of dollars for this jewelry while sacrificing to make those weekly payments. However, Cash for Gold only gave me a check for $150. I wish I had known this before sending it to them. In my desperation, I did not even ask. The package also included my 18k gold high school graduation ring and any loose gold I found in my jewelry box.

My jaw dropped to the floor when I opened the envelope, thinking I was going to get at least a thousand dollars. I deposited the check in the bank and moved on. As sad as I was, I did not cry over spilled milk. I have a bigger fish to fry, as they say; move on, Egli, move on.

Mommy Egli

July 23, 2008, 12:11 a.m.
Day 101 on our road to recovery

Dear Companions on our journey,

Natalia is officially a teen; her many birthday celebrations were a blast! We had a fantastic time, and we thank you for the birthday wishes, prayers, kindness, and generosity. Please know that your thoughtfulness is greatly appreciated.

Birthday festivities started last Tuesday with a mommy and daughter picnic at Prospect Park, followed by a family day at the Bronx Zoo on Wednesday, a special celebration with our community of faith on Thursday and her actual birthday, Friday, July 18th, we were invited to the Good Morning America show to see Miley Cyrus also known as Hannah Montana. Natalia got a special birthday hug from cancer survivor, Robin Roberts. We then had a special lunch with my goddaughter Isabella and niece, Dariela, who also joined us for the show. We ended the day with a fabulous family dinner at Carmine's with my friend Steve. On Saturday, her birthday festivities continued. We had an all-day BBQ with family and friends at Prospect Park, followed by a slumber party with cousins and friends Kim, Dariela, Briana and Mayte. Festivities ended with a quiet mother-daughter dinner on Sunday evening.

We really know how to party; the whole week was filled with joy and laughter. This is very symbolic of how Natalia and I live. Each day we celebrate life and one another. Natalia has been loved and celebrated from the moment she was in my womb. Every summer, her birthday celebrations turn into a birthday marathon of festivities, and this year was no exception. Even in our moments of darkness, we never see the glass half empty. We always find a reason to celebrate.

My star is enjoying being a teenager. Since last Sunday she has been delighting us with Karaoke on her PlayStation, one of her birthday gifts. Even now, as I write, she is singing in the background and telling me, "I have to dance and party up before I go into surgery, mommy." I know her dance teacher Lauren, will be happy to know that even under these circumstances, Natalia is still dancing.

On a more serious note, I met with Natalia's care team at Memorial Sloan Kettering yesterday, and as of now the surgery scheduled for this Thursday is on hold due to a rash Natalia developed on her cheek that looks like shingles. I took her to the hospital early this morning again and they will determine what the next step will be.

In the meantime, thank you for walking this path with us. I ask you to please continue to carry us close to your heart and let God's will be done. Pray for us, send us blessings, peace, healing and stillness. I am shaking in my pants. I am so nervous as the day gets closer. I know that this too shall pass. The earth is ours to enjoy and we trust that our lives are in divine order by the grace of God.

Natalia's courage and self-esteem are so admirable. She no longer covers her head to go out. She walks around bald with her head up high and a big bright smile on her face. Papi calls her *mi pelona* and he is continually kissing her bald head as I put lots of sunblock on it to protect it.

With the most profound love and gratitude,
Egli

Natalia celebrating her thirteenth birthday in Prospect Park, Brooklyn, a week before the major leg reconstruction.

July 23, 2008, 8:57 p.m.
This is still day 101 on our road to recovery

Dear Faithful Companions,

After spending a long morning in an isolation room at the hospital, the physicians decided that Natalia's rash was not shingles and we are proceeding with the procedure as planned. The surgery will be done tomorrow, July 24th and I am so scared.

This afternoon, we had all the pre-operation work done and are almost ready to go. I took a break from packing our hospital bags to write these lines and try to process the emotional rollercoaster we have been through. Please continue to pray for Natalia's continued recovery. We are calm before the storm and confident that all is already well. She is relaxed and very informed of what will happen during and after surgery.

Yesterday, when we met with the orthopedic surgeon, Natalia asked to see the prosthesis she is getting, and we were in shock at the size and weight of it. We were not aware that she was also getting a knee replacement. When she was initially diagnosed, the surgeon was happy that the knee was cancer-free, but to replace the distal femur where the 16-centimeter tumor is, it needs to be attached to the knee. It took me a while to process this new information. I almost passed out, but after the lengthy meetings and conversations with the team yesterday and today, things make a lot more sense. The other option is to amputate the leg and that is unthinkable for us. It has been a lot of information to absorb and things to learn and process in 101 days.

We were informed that the procedure will last

about six hours – three hours to remove the tumor and another three hours to reconstruct the leg. The incision will be about 18 inches long on the inner thigh.

We are leaving home at 5:00 a.m. to be at the hospital by 6:00 a.m. The procedure is scheduled to begin at 7:00 a.m. My community of faith have designated tomorrow as a day of prayer and fasting for Natalia.

It is raining cats and dogs now; the loud thunder and lightning make our room look like a disco. Jenny just came into the room to remind me that it is raining just as hard as the night Natalia was born. I find this very symbolic of the new life she and we will begin tomorrow.

In advance, I give thanks to God for Natalia's healing. I know deep in my heart that this too shall pass and pretty soon she is going to be dancing on two feet again. I still have more packing to do and Natalia is calling me to clip her toenails.

With much love and gratitude for Natalia's healing,
Egli

Egli Colón Stephens, Ed.D.

CHAPTER 10
I PRAYED TO MY GOD FOR HELP

In my distress I called to the Lord; I cried to my God for help. From his temple he heard my voice; my cry came before him, into his ears.
  - **Psalm 18:6**

Life is this simple: we are living in a world that is absolutely transparent, and the divine is shining through it all the time. This is not just a nice story or a fable, it is true.
  - **Thomas Merton**

July 24, 2008, 9:50 a.m.
Day 101 on our road to recovery

Dear Faithful Companions,

This is the day we have been waiting for so anxiously. Natalia has been in the operating room since 7:48 a.m. She was sitting up on the stretcher, waving to us before the doors of the operating room closed. Her dad and her Nana came to see her off. I kept it together as much as I could to keep her strong, but I was scared. We all surrounded her in a circle and prayed together, but right before she went in, her dad broke down. He could not resist the pain we were both feeling seeing our little girl go through such horror.

Natalia continues to be stoic and strong. She resisted the sedatives offered by the anesthesiologist before going into the operating room in fear of missing anything. Some things don't change! She has been the same since birth; she always resisted bedtime in fear of missing anything during her sleep, I guess. A few minutes before going in, the team came around again and this time she asked them to give her what they had offered before, to take the edge off.

She was laughing and being her goofy self as we were rolling the stretcher as far as we could to the operating room. I did not want to let go of it, but I am trusting that God will be with the physicians operating on her and they will return a cancer-free child to me.

The family is now gathered in the waiting area and I am in the chapel down the hall. Time is going by really slow, and in this moment of impatience and desperation, I turn to You my God. I am feeling numb, and my heart is aching as I imagine what is happening to my child behind the closed doors of the operating room. The surgeon started to remove the tumor at 9:10 a.m. Nurse Cunningham comes by periodically to let us know what is happening in there. I am so appreciative of these updates. We find comfort in one another and simply being still in silence while we wait for more updates, knowing that God's grace is comforting us and restoring Natalia to health and wholeness.

Seeking God's peace and comfort,
Egli

July 24, 2008, 1:28 p.m.
Day 102 still on our road to recovery (in surgery)

At 1:22 p.m., nurse Cunningham informed me that the orthopedic surgeon had successfully removed all cancerous tissues, bone (femur), muscles and was starting the reconstruction of the leg. Surgery is expected to end at about 4:00 p.m. This is a lot longer than what they had anticipated.

Please continue to pray for us; we are connected in spirit.

Trusting in God's loving power,
Egli

July 24, 2008, 5:18 p.m.
Day 102 still on our road to recovery

The surgery was a complete success! Thank You, Jesus!

Natalia came out of the operating room at around 4:00 p.m. She is now in the recovery room preparing to have a blood transfusion because of all the lost blood during the procedures.

I just spent some time holding her hand and comforting her. Her leg hurts a lot and she is moaning in pain. I was informed that the pain management team were not expecting her to be so tall for an average 13-year-old and did not order enough pain medication. They are taking care of this now.

This is all for today, I will remain by her side and attentive to her needs. Oh, how I wish I could spare her this pain and discomfort.
Spirit of the living Christ, please continue to embrace us in Your arms.

Mommy Egli

July 25, 2008, 1:28 p.m.
Day 103 on our road to recovery

This is Natalia's aunt, Jenny bringing you today's update. Natalia is stable and recovering wonderfully.

Egli is too tired and emotionally drained to write but wants to thank you for your continued prayers and we will keep you updated.

Our soldier is a true trooper!
Jen

July 27, 2008, 11:17 p.m.
Day 105 on our road to recovery

Hello Family and Friends,

This is Natalia. It has been three days since the big surgery, and I am bouncing back. I took my first steps the day after surgery. I was really scared, but with the help of the physical therapist, Megan and my mom, I managed to get out of bed and take a few steps down the hall. I almost went all around the floor, but I was a little dizzy. I don't remember my first steps as a baby, so it felt amazing to witness this moment. I was a bit wobbly and of course, holding on to mommy and Megan as they pushed the IV poles and all the tubes connected to me. I am still not ready to walk on my own.

Natalia, the day after the first leg reconstruction taking her first steps.

Thanks for all the supportive messages you have sent. I look at my guestbook as much as I can and I am surprised at all the people that sign in to say that they are rooting for me. I have made friends all over the world.

It is about 11:19 p.m. right now, and it is day 104 on our road to recovery, this all seems so surreal to me still. This morning when the surgery team came to do rounds, they removed the bandages, and I got to see my stitches. The incision is huge; it looks like a snake. The doctors do their rounds very early, and they don't let me sleep much around here. A parade of doctors in white coats surrounded my bed at around 6:00 a.m. and woke up mommy and I. Mommy sleeps in a cot next to my bed and we get to hold hands most of the night; she never lets me go.

I am not an early bird. I did not even get a chance to open my eyes fully before doctors started peeling the bandages off my leg so abruptly. I was annoyed because, for a minute, I forgot where I was. Mommy sat up and looked startled too. They said they were going to come in every morning, and I am not looking forward to that.

I will try to write tomorrow if I can, and tell you how everything is going.

I had a lot of visitors today at the hospital. My family comes every day. Daddy, Nana, Mami Lula, Papi, Titi Jenny, my little cousin - Dariela, and my mom who stays with me 24 hours a day. Also, my uncle Claudio visited with my aunt, Miosotis and my cousins Kimberly and Kevin. Oh, and I can't forget our friend, Joe also came today. It was truly a Sunday Funday.

Thanks for making me feel so special.
Alrighty then, see ya later!
Natalia

August 4, 2008, 3:40 a.m.
Day 113 on our road to recovery

Dear Faithful Companions,

I have been at a loss for words or perhaps too tired, physically, mentally and emotionally. My spirit has sustained me and all I can say is that our God is awesome. I keep believing wholeheartedly that all will be well and in divine order.

Natalia was discharged from the hospital on Friday and is recovering beautifully. Our lives continue to be filled with blessings and miracles, and we give God thanks and praise.

We closed on our condo in Harlem on Friday, August 1st and are now in the process of moving. I longed to be a homeowner again, and it never happened when I desperately wanted it to happen. I never gave up on this dream and kept saving every penny I could. This milestone is truly the definition of a miracle. God is making a way out of no way. When the market crashed earlier this year, and our world collapsed, I had my life's savings all invested in this property. We encountered many obstacles along the way, but the keys are in our hands already. This has truly been a lesson to trust God's timing and plans for our lives.

My parents met me at the hospital early on Friday. Papi and I went to Sovereign Bank, now Santander near 59th Street, to cash out my Roth IRA and get the final checks for the closing. Mami stayed at the hospital with Natalia. They expressed how proud they are of me. *Mi hija lograstes el sueño Americano.* Mami brought me my seersucker suit for the closing, and I showered and changed quickly in the patient's bathroom. Papi looked sharp too. He decided he was going to accompany me everywhere that day.

"I am your bodyguard," He said.

He was as excited as I was. We walked side by side to the bank and joked around. It felt good to get out of the hospital for a bit, laugh and walk in the congested streets of midtown. My attorney and friend, Sonja waited for us at the property's office somewhere in the Wall Street area. She is Natalia's cousin and a woman of deep faith. Before we got on the elevator, she said, "Let us go into this corner and pray." It was comforting to hear her invoke God's presence into the transaction that was about to take place. It all seemed so surreal for me. Our lives had changed drastically since we started this process in 2006. As excited as I was for what was about to happen, my priorities had changed and this became something else I would get to cross off my bucket list.

Every Friday after work, I would pick up Natalia from school and drive to the construction site a few blocks away. We would get out of the car and watch from across the street the workers diligently stack one brick on top of the other. One Friday, when there weren't too many workers, I came closer and stood on the grounds. I stood there in silence for a few minutes and prayed. Dear God, protect the workers, bless the families that one day will inhabit this building and I thank You in advance for the beautiful memories we are going to create here. Once again, You have exceeded my expectations.

There were tons of bricks nicely stacked up on the sidewalk, ready to be put up. Before I walked away, I took one with me and kept it on our coffee table as a centerpiece, right next to the floor plan. I prayed over our new home before we set foot in it.

I had bittersweet feelings on the day of the closing. I was sad for my girl and all that had transpired in just two years; I would never have thought that our lives would take such a drastic turn. I never imagined that I would be leaving for the closing of my property from my daughter's hospital room.

This weekend, we also experienced another miracle, our dog was found. Princess ran away from home a week ago while Natalia was in the hospital. My mom left the gate door open by mistake and our dog walked out. We were told that she was last seen at the corner and that the mailman had picked her up and given her away to a lady passing by. We have been on a mission to get Princess back before Natalia gets discharged from the hospital. They are inseparable.

We broke the news to Natalia the night before coming home. I was nervous about telling her; I thought she was going to have a nervous breakdown, jump out of bed and hurt her leg. I told her nurse and doctor to stay in the room with me while I told her in case they had to sedate her. To my surprise she took the news well, her eyes swelled up, but the first words out of her mouth were, "I am going to find her; she is going to come back." Her certainty and serene attitude shocked me.

We were doing everything we could to find her. Jenny was on a mission to find Princess and had brought all her friends on board. They placed posters with a current picture of Natalia with Princess explaining her condition and offering a reward to whoever returned her. Jenny and her crew went as far as placing posters into the buildings and elevators in our neighborhood with the hope that the story would touch the hearts of those who have Princess to return her.

The same night we told Natalia, we started to get phone calls with lead information. Natalia's faith was steadfast; she was still convinced that we were going to find Princess. Some calls were false alarms or inaccurate information, but a couple of days later a lady called offering to return the dog. She said we could come over to see her.

They had purchased a new wardrobe, bowls and leash for her. Her sons were taking good care of her and she said Princess had brought much joy to their home. My sister went to identify Princess and it was her. She was happy in her new-found home, but she was ecstatic when she saw Jenny.

They had also named her Princess, they said they tried calling her other names, but she got excited and responded when she was called Princess. The lady refused to accept a reward and gave us all the beautiful things she had purchased for Princess. This family lives only a few blocks away from my parents. We offered them joint custody and invited them to come to visit her whenever they wanted to.

We sent the mom a beautiful thank you gift as a token of our gratitude.

Natalia is thrilled to have her doggy back and is ready to move into her new home. This is another manifestation brought to life. We have been creating vision boards with images of how we are going to decorate each room. She wants to paint her room hot pink with black borders and gold stripes and zebra bedding in the same colors. I hope I can bring her dream room to life. I am sure I will.

Much love and gratitude to all,
Egli

August 6, 2008, 5:15 p.m.
Day 115 on our road to recovery

Dear faithful companions,

Things have taken a different turn. As I write these lines to you, Natalia is having surgery again on the same leg to vacuum a hematoma. She has been bleeding a lot since Monday, I kept changing the bandages frequently, but I did not see any progress. Something just did not feel right and I decided to rush her back to the hospital. We are now in the waiting area, both grandmas, her dad, titi Jenny, niece Dariela and I are patiently waiting.

Natalia was cheerful as the stretcher was being wheeled into the operating room. She was sitting up, smiling and waving her hand at us. Her spirit is untouchable and for this and so much more, I give God thanks and praise.

We were told that this was not going to be a lengthy operation and not long ago, were informed that they are beginning to close up the incision. She should be in the recovery room soon. In the midst of it all, we give thanks to God for His mercy and for providing Natalia with excellent medical care.

Please continue to pray for us and send us your healing blessings.

In peace and hope,
Egli

August 7, 2008, 4:52 a.m.
Day 116 on our road to wholeness and wellness

Dear faithful companions,

By God's divine grace, all is well. The procedure was not as long and complicated as the other one. The orthopedic surgeon did not have to remove the prosthesis or re-open the previous 18-inch incision to remove the hematoma, but enlarged another small incision Natalia had behind the knee to vacuum the hematoma.

Natalia is recovering well, she did not stay long in the recovery area, and we were transferred to a room in pediatrics. Unfortunately, we are becoming popular on the floor and were received with a warm welcome.

Natalia woke up from surgery very hungry, asking for food. As soon as she got the ok to eat, she asked for sushi at 10:00 p.m. I did not have to go far for it because the hospital cafeteria had fresh sushi but not miso soup.

All is well and in divine order, this is only a little bump on our road to recovery, but we are healed in the Name of Jesus and nothing is going to take our joy away. We embrace what it is and surrender it all to the almighty, *Dios todo lo puede*.

In peace and love,
Egli

P.S. Natalia is sleeping peacefully when she is not being interrupted by physicians, nurses or aides for vital signs, blood work, urine and more. She keeps telling them to let her sleep and be quiet, "Ssshh."

August 9, 2008, 9:24 a.m.
Day 118 on our road to recovery

Dear faithful cyber companions,

Thank you very much for walking this journey with us and for your faithful prayers. Thank God for technology! We feel your presence with us and your words of encouragement inspire us to keep on going strong.

All continues to be well and in divine order. We are at our new home for the weekend and we resume cycle seven of chemo this Monday, August 11th at 7:00 a.m. Natalia has been off chemo for almost a month, so it will be quite a challenge to start all over again. She even grew some fuzz; her head looks like a delicious Georgia peach, and we can't stop kissing it.

This time, our stay in the hospital was shorter. Natalia was out of bed the day after surgery again, walking down the hall on crutches with the physical therapist. It is amazing to see her take her first steps and almost feels like when she was learning how to walk around the age of ten months. As you can imagine, I am right behind her, ready to catch her and with the camcorder on the other hand, recording every bit.

We are not looking forward to returning to chemotherapy this Monday. We have thirteen more cycles to go, intense physical and occupational therapy in addition to a long healing process of both surgeries.

The road ahead seems difficult, but we continue to lean on God and take things one day at the time. We are very thankful to be surrounded by a fantastic family, friends and a great team of caregivers.

As I write, I am watching Natalia sleep peacefully, and she brings comfort to my aching heart.

Much love and peace from our new home in Harlem.
Egli

P.S. I am going to do some unpacking while she is still asleep. We are living out of boxes. By the way, her bright pink room is coming along just great, but I need sunglasses to get in there, that is how bright and cheerful it is; just like my girl!

August 11, 2008, 6:18 p.m.
Day 120 on our road to recovery

Dear Faithful Companions,

It is 6:20 p.m., we are getting ready to leave the hospital and return tomorrow morning. Natalia is being sent home with the chemo IV on a backpack. Usually, they send us home with clear IV fluids for hydration, but I was told the approach has changed.

She was given medication to ease the side effects, but they have not kicked in yet. She is still not feeling well. Her body has been chemo free for a few weeks now and I guess it feels like an invasion. Natalia is upset about having to do this again. She is crying and asking for her life to be the way it was before the diagnosis. I told her crying and complaining is allowed, but quitting is not an option. It hurts me to have to be so stern with her, but I need to keep her focused.

The night ahead will be a long one, but the sun will rise in the morning and bring new hope.

Hurting mama,
Egli

August 12, 2008, 4:52 p.m.
Day 121 on our road to recovery

Dear Faithful Companions,

The sun rose again for me this morning after a long night. It is almost setting now and our day at the hospital is almost ending. We got through another rough day. Tomorrow's sunrise will bring us closer to the end of this cycle and like everything in life, this too shall pass. This too shall end and one day, will be a distant memory.

Natalia was sedated most of the day; when she is awake, she is in a lot of discomfort from the chemo side effects. We are going home again with chemo and IV fluids in a backpack. Both grandmas and her dad just arrived. Both grandmas, Nana and Mami Lula, brought Natalia tamarind balls: this acidic tropical fruit sold in our highly populated Caribbean neighborhood brings her comfort. They are both laughing because they both brought the same thing at the same time without knowing. I call that the gift of love and a grandmother's intuition. Their desire to comfort Natalia drives them to synchronize telepathically with her desires.

Peace and love,
Egli

August 14, 2008, 4:43 p.m.
Day 123 on our road to recovery

Dear Faithful Companions,

I thank you so much for fighting a good fight with us. This has been a brutal week for Natalia, for lack of a better word. The chemo is really kicking our butts and we are kicking back. We have been knocked to the ground a couple of times, but we have bounced back.

Unfortunately, Natalia has had ongoing treatments this whole week. I have taken her home from the hospital with a chemo IV in the backpack to run overnight along with IV fluids to keep her hydrated for the past four days. The reason for this new method is because there is a shortage of the medication that was given to her to protect her heart. They give her the condensed chemo on one day and spend the rest of the days hydrating her to get the toxins out. I hope this makes sense; I am repeating what we were told and praying for my daughter's well-being.

I am in complete anguish and desperation with all we have gone through this week. We have been feeling all kinds of intense emotions. I have even offered the hospital to pay out of pocket and contact the manufacturer to get this medication, but their response has been: "The shortage is worldwide."

There are so many children here suffering and they are doing everything they can. They keep assuring us the alternative method they are doing is safe. It upsets me even more
that we have made a regression.

As of now, there is no word of when this medication will be available to us. Let us pray, my dear friends to the God we know, a God of love, justice, and mercy. A God that makes the impossible possible. Natalia will need this medication in a couple of months again as well as the other patients here.

We were hoping for this to be a short week, but we have to return to the hospital tomorrow considering all the complications we had. We are now being sent home with another backpack of IV fluids to continue flushing the toxins out. In addition to all of the nonsense we are going through, Natalia had to be re-accessed yesterday because her chest port line, the Mediport, was clogged.

This little girl has gone through so much that she is beginning to say she wants to quit, again. She is upset, frustrated, and sad, and does not want to go on.

Please continue to pray for us, send us positive healing energy so that we do not get distracted and weak from all the negative things that are happening around us and to us. To top it off, Natalia was exposed to Chickenpox by her roommate last week, so for the next 10-15 days, we need to be seen in an isolation room through Urgent Care.

Ay caramba, when it rains, it pours!

I am ending this journal entry with a smile. I am hoping for more rainbows in our lives. This too shall pass. We need to keep pushing, fighting, hoping, loving and believing.

With the most profound gratitude, love and friendship,
Egli - Proud mommy of a warrior.

P.S. Thanks for your support and companionship during these dark and stormy days.

August 15, 2008, 9:39 p.m.
Day 124 on our road to recovery

Dear Faithful Companions,

We are home now, thank God. We made it through another brutal cycle. My warrior is now resting and she sends her love.

This was a tough one. Next week Natalia's blood counts are expected to drop and she would be at high risk for infection. Once again, we are going to stay optimistic and hold on to our faith.

For now, we are going to focus on replenishing ourselves. Natalia will begin physical therapy this Monday again; there are no breaks in this marathon.

Chemo cycle number eight is in two weeks. She will receive three consecutive cycles of Methotrexate.

Thanks for lifting us in prayers and encouraging us to make it to the finish line. We did it!

Paz y Esperanza,
Egli

August 17, 2008, 4:10 p.m.
Day 126 on our Olympic marathon to recovery

Dear Faithful Companions,

We were hoping for this to be a peaceful and uneventful weekend, but yesterday morning I had to rush Natalia to the emergency department at Memorial Sloan Kettering for shortness of breath, chest and stomach pains. This was scary; I thought she had a heart attack. The Echocardiogram, X-rays and blood work were fine, thank God. Apparently, her blood pressure dropped. She still feels weak and is experiencing shortness of breath when she tries to sit up in bed, but we are home. We are in our new home in Harlem; just her and I.

Got to go, she is calling me and her voice gets louder by the second. She asked me to get her a little bell to call for me when I am not next to her. Isn't she funny? Who does she think I am? Hazel, the maid?

Thank you very much for all you do for us. Your kindness, encouragement and generosity are greatly appreciated.

Egli

August 21, 2008, 7:49 a.m.
Day 130 on our journey to wellness and wholeness

Dear Companions,

This morning I write to you from an isolation room in the emergency department at the hospital. Natalia had to be admitted yesterday afternoon with a high fever, vomiting and with very low blood pressure.

When I brought her in for her checkup on Tuesday, her blood counts were low, but they allowed me to take her home. We got to spend 22 hours at home and Natalia even got to make mini pancakes on her own yesterday morning for breakfast. She felt weak but insisted on making them. She sat on the marble counter with her leg up on pillows. She is now stable but continues to be neutropenic, meaning that her germ-fighting cells (white blood cells) are very low. We are waiting to be transferred to our own room. The pediatric floor is packed and we may be transferred to a regular floor. Many of the children that were on treatment with her last week are here, sick as well, so I am wondering if the shortage of the medication has anything to do with this. This is something to think and pray about.

Overall, Natalia has been in good spirits for most of the week. Her Nana came over on Monday, and they got to spend a lot of quality time making their family tree. Natalia has been in bed for the most part; she is too weak to walk on her crutches. We had to put off the physical therapy.

Again, many thanks for walking this journey with us and carrying us close to your hearts. Your prayers, words of encouragement and generosity are greatly appreciated.

In the hope of brighter and better days,
Egli - Proud mom of a true warrior.

August 22, 2008, 11:04 a.m.
Day 131 on the battlefield

Dear Soldiers,

    We are still in combat. Our warrior Natalia is still fighting a good fight. We are at the hospital, feeling like prisoners in this isolation room, but we are in good spirits. I am here, next to Natalia and following her orders. I am following every command from the commander in chief.

    On another note, I write to you today from a different cell. We were transferred yesterday afternoon to a high floor, so high we can almost touch the sky. We are still captive in an isolation room, but we are happy to have a window to look out. The cars going up and down York Avenue look like toys from such a high floor.

    Our warrior's condition is stable but very little change. Her white blood cells' count is still low and to top it off, she got a bad cold. She is congested but manages to breathe through her mouth. The decongestants are not helping much. If she would only let me get my eucalyptus and peppermint oil or some Vicks Vapor Rub, I would take care of that, but she doesn't let me leave her side at all. I don't blame her, we are on an unfamiliar floor and the room is not as bright and beautiful as on the pediatric floor.

    She just had a back and foot massage by a wonderful lady from the Integrated Medicine Department and is now sipping on some tea with honey. I am glad this hospital has a whole building dedicated to a more holistic approach to medicine. We are combining both, the traditional and holistic in the hopes to alleviate Natalia's condition. I was surprised when they came to our room. I usually take her out for full body massages a few blocks away from the hospital. This was a sweet treat at a time greatly needed.

Thank you very much for your prayers, love and words of encouragement.

En la lucha,
Egli

August 23, 2008, 10:51 p.m.
Day 132 on our road to recovery

Dear Faithful Companions,

Natalia was discharged early this evening. Her white blood cells count went up from 0.2 to 3.8.

Our God is a miraculous God. It feels great to be home, our new home is our sanctuary. It embraces us with a warmth, unlike any other.

Natalia is in great spirits; the stitches from both surgeries were removed yesterday. The incisions are healing nicely and she doesn't seem bothered with the scars. Her virus is also going away and she no longer has a fever.

In faith, love and hope,
Egli

Egli Colón Stephens, Ed.D.

CHAPTER 11
LET YOUR SPIRIT DANCE

Let them praise his name with dancing and make music to him with timbrel and harp.
    - Psalm 149:3

Dance, when you are broken open. Dance, if you have torn the bandage off. Dance in the middle of the fighting. Dance in your blood. Dance when you are perfectly free.
    - Rumi

September 2, 2008, 8:22 a.m.
Day 142 on our road to recovery

Dear Friends,

Unlike many children who begin their first day of school today in New York City, we are embarking on a different journey. We are back at the hospital for three consecutive weeks of chemo.

Natalia would have been starting eighth grade at The Young Women's Leadership School in East Harlem, instead, she will attend school at the hospital and will be home schooled when she is no longer on treatment.

She completed the rest of seventh grade at the hospital when she was first diagnosed in April. It has been a balancing act, but we remain faithful and hopeful.

This too shall pass.

En amor y esperanza,
Egli

September 5, 2008, 12:14 p.m.
Day 145 on our road to recovery

Dear Soldiers,

As I write to you on this sunny Friday afternoon, we are concluding cycle eight of chemo and have eleven more to go.

Natalia responded very well to this round. She had the usual side effects, but we got through them. Her appetite was good; she was craving a lot of Mexican and Japanese food but retaining very little.

She has been talking and thinking a lot about school this week. Each night, on our way home, she has asked me to drive by her school. She is redefining normal and somewhat adapting to receiving school lessons by her bedside at the hospital or at home.

Natalia is excited about the eighth grade and has been bombarding her teacher with questions and telling him how things should be done with her.

Our favorite nurse, Christie just came in and told us that we are discharged. Hooray! Natalia is being disconnected from the IVs and is rushing me to get her out of here. We have to be back on Monday for two more weeks of chemo.

We made it through the week, God is good, and for that, we are eternally grateful.

Today is her Nana's seventy-something birthday. Natalia wants me to take her to Brooklyn to surprise Nana with flowers. My daughter's thoughtfulness amazes me. I am glad she can think of others in the midst of her situation.

Abrazos,
Egli

September 8, 2008, 1:07 p.m.
Day 148 on our road to recovery

Dear Faithful Companions,
    We had a pleasant and restful weekend and even made it to church yesterday. We are back at the hospital to begin cycle nine and Natalia is fighting a good fight. She is in great spirits and just now, she went to the teen lounge to play while the chemo IV runs through her all day. I know that shortly she will be back here in her room, knocked out by the horrible side effects. It gives me great joy to know she is playing and interacting with other teens dealing with cancer as well.
    Natalia's orthopedic surgeon, stopped by this morning. She says her prognosis looks good. She is now able to bend her knee and put more weight on her leg but needs to work on straightening and lifting her leg. She also said that in a few months, Natalia would be walking on her own without the crutches. It has been challenging to start physical therapy since the surgery because she has been too sick from the treatments. We know we have much work ahead, but it is exciting to know that she is making progress.
    I have a special request: Natalia loves to hear baby stories of herself or any childhood memories. I am running out of stories to tell her and don't want to make up any. So, I am asking you to please, write to us any memories you may have from when she was younger or how you met her. Our days are long and going down memory lane will bring some laughter to us.
    We are looking forward to reminiscing with you.

Con mucho amor y esperanza,
Egli - Proud mommy of a true warrior.

September 11, 2008, 9:42 a.m.
Day 151 on our road to recovery

Dear Faithful Companions,

Natalia continues to be in great spirits and fighting a good fight. She is responding well to this week's treatments, and we are glad this week is almost over. We don't even want to think about next week's treatment. We were told to expect the worst. The anticipation can be paralyzing, but we are staying in the present moment as much as possible. We are focusing our energy on how far we have come and all we have accomplished with God's grace.

I am now sitting outside Natalia's room while she is working with her teacher, Ross on some math problems that I don't have a clue about. I am glad that I am just mom for now, and that is quite enough. My priorities have changed and these days, I don't push the academics as much. Natalia has been managing to keep up with the school work and eighth grade is going well.

She is finally looking forward to a good night's sleep without my interruptions every few hours to give her tons of medication and to measure her pH level. We have not had a good night sleep in almost two weeks.

Thank you very much for going down memory lane with us and sharing your memories of Natalia. Keep them coming! They have been enjoyable to read, however, remember that they don't have to be elaborate when you write them; I am not grading you on it.

Much love and peace today on 9-11, a day we remember as being invaded, attacked and so much more. A year from now, I want to remember 9-11-

08 as a day that I witnessed my warrior fighting a battle to live and won. Natalia has taught me the true meaning of courage, strength, resilience and hope. A day does not go by without her finding a reason to smile and give thanks. She has truly embraced this hospital's community and often expresses her gratitude to them.

En la paz de Dios,
Egli - Proud mommy of a true warrior.

September 16, 2008, 8:49 a.m.
Day 156 on our road to recovery

Dear faithful companions,

Thank you very much for your continuous love, prayers, and support. Natalia is in great spirits, but she is not feeling too well physically. Again, this week's treatments had to be postponed until next week, again, due to numerous mouth sores from the past two consecutive weeks of treatments.

We are taking advantage of this week to heal a bit, catch up with school work, unpack some more and go back to physical therapy to strengthen "Will" with "Grace."

For those who don't remember, Natalia named the leg with the former tumor "Will," that it "will get better," so I named the other leg "Grace" after one of my favorite TV shows, Will and Grace, but more importantly, because it is by the grace of God that my daughter will soon heal and walk again.

In God's will and grace,
Egli

**September 22, 2008, 6:18 p.m.
Day 162 on our road to recovery**

Dear Companions,

Happy first day of fall to all and thank you very much for walking this road with us. We are back at the hospital for another round of chemo this week. Natalia is in great spirits and determined to beat the brutal side effects. She wants to stay awake and push herself to the classroom and the teen lounge as much as possible. Today, she was very successful at it, although she was attached to three IV pumps. She got out of the room, and we even took part in a mini fall parade here at the hospital.

The sun is almost setting on the Upper East Side and Natalia is sleeping until we are sent home for the night with a chemo IV. There is still a shortage of the medication that helps protect the heart and run the chemo faster. Instead, I have been told that the chemo is now running for 72 hours to protect the heart.

A close friend of ours was able to get the medication for us at another hospital, but our hospital refused to accept it. We were now told that the only company that makes this medication is not making it anymore until the FDA approves it. Apparently, it has to do with the cost of making it. We live in such a capitalist society! – I am so frustrated.

Last week was great. She worked hard in physical therapy to prepare for an upcoming masquerade party and fundraiser that my Vermont sisters are giving in her honor on October 18th at Transfiguration church hall in Brooklyn. Her wish is to be able to stand without crutches next month and hopefully, to dance. I am looking forward to dancing with my daughter.

We were just told we are going home for the night. Thank You God for always looking out for us. There's no better place than home.

With much love and gratitude for your unconditional support, love and prayers,
Egli

September 27, 2008, 12:36 p.m.
Day 167 on our road to recovery

Dear Soldiers,

This has been an intense week for Natalia. As expected, she had Cisplatin (chemo) running through her veins day and night for 72 hours. The last drop went in at 12:04 p.m. on Thursday and yesterday (Friday), we went into the hospital to get IV hydration.

Unfortunately, Natalia could not do all the things she wanted to do this week, like take her daily lessons and go into the teen lounge at the hospital. She had to be heavily sedated most of the week to handle the side effects which were brutal as usual.

This week, we were also informed that this chemo is one of the most toxic ones. It affected her hearing and as a result, she lost some of her hearing frequency. At the beginning of the treatment, we were told that this was a possibility, but our priority has been to get the cancer under control.

Natalia can still hear well and as of now, there is no need for a hearing aid, but this bothers me a lot. This is my child, and I want all of her to be well.

On July 18th, 1995, at 3:30 a.m. I gave birth to a perfectly healthy, 7 pounds, 3 ounces, $20\frac{1}{2}$ inches long baby girl named Natalia at Long Island Jewish Hospital. I have taken care of my baby girl as my most precious treasure and in these past 166 days, seeing her health crumble has been a nightmare.

There is still beauty, wholeness and wellness in my daughter. This week, 160 plus days later reality hit me and it hit me hard. I have been sad. We are more than halfway through this journey, but I guess I have been on autopilot. I have been on survival mode, doing what we need to do to keep on going. Seeing her so sick this week, sedated for the most part and not having her respond to my voice has left a void in my heart. I am keeping my eyes focused on the final prize, which is having my daughter healthy again and living a day at a time without the fear that this cancer may attack our lives again. At times, I ask myself how much more can we endure? This is frightening and I am feeling weak. In my weakness, Lord, I come to you for strength. Hold us tight dear God.

This week we have also been told that only 30% of the tumor was dead or shrunk before the surgery. In other words, the six rounds of chemo before surgery only killed 30% of the tumor. Thankfully, they were able to remove it all at the time of surgery.

My hope, their hope and prayer is that the remaining rounds of chemo will eliminate any cancerous cells that may have spread throughout her body. We just finished round ten yesterday and we have nine more rounds to go.

In the meantime, Natalia is resting on the couch. Yes, we now have a new couch in our new place. I had to convince myself that it was okay to splurge on a couch only because I don't want Natalia to come from a hospital bed to another bed in her room. We are off from chemo for the next two weeks. She is expected to be neutropenic in the next few days, that is when white blood cells drop, and she is prone to infections. Let us pray that there will be no hospitalization this time; we are really enjoying our new condo and couch.

We are so looking forward to getting some rest, recovering and regaining the strength to continue on our journey. This has been a tiring month.

Got to go now, Natalia is asking for rice and beans. This will be her first meal since last Monday.

Thank you very much for taking the time to read this lengthy journal entry and letting me vent my fears, frustrations, pain, and hopes.

Con amor y esperanza,
Egli - Proud mommy of a warrior named Natalia.

October 1, 2008, 9:20 p.m.
Day 171 on our road to recovery

My Dear Companions,

When I woke up this morning, the first thought and word that came to mind was gratitude. As I am getting ready to end this day, I would like to end it by giving thanks to God for blessing us with loving, supportive and generous friends. It makes a tremendous difference to know that we have an outstanding team out there cheering us on and doing so much for us. The list of whom we should thank is endless, but you know who you are.

It is so hard for me to be on the receiving end. It is so much easier to give, love, care and support others, but I must say one of the hardest and greatest lessons I am learning in this whole ordeal is to open my arms and receive. As a parent, I have taught Natalia to embrace life with courage. I have told her from a young age that life does not owe us anything, to embrace each day with determination and gratitude, and to make the best of it. So, it is very humbling for us to be where we are.

I am overwhelmed with the outpouring of love, kindness, and generosity. I need you to know that Natalia and I are incredibly thankful and feel privileged to know how much we are loved.

In the midst of all the chaos in this world, God's goodness is greater. All of you are a testament to God's love and you make this world and ours, a better place. So, from the very bottom of our mending hearts, Natalia and I would like to say, *gracias, muchas gracias*, for blessing us with your presence in our lives.

On a different note, but also one of gratitude, Natalia got through another day here at home.

Yesterday, I took her for her checkup and to physical therapy. She is not doing too well on paper but is in great spirits. She is neutropenic; her white blood cells dropped below average and she only has God's grace to protect her from any infections. Her red blood cells, hemoglobin, hematocrit, and platelets are low, but physicians are waiting until Friday for the possibility of another blood transfusion.

Despite the adversities, Natalia woke up this morning with her mind set on baking, so she made it to the kitchen with her crutches, sat on a stool in front of the counter and baked some cinnamon cookies and a little cake with the leftover dough. She was gasping for air as she was mixing the ingredients but got to put them in the oven and then collapsed on the couch, ready to quit her desires to be a pastry chef. She then insisted on having me taste her experiment and all I can say is that I am still living. With that said, I don't know if I want another cookie. They are all still looking pretty on a plate and I now have a huge mess in the kitchen to clean up.

Thank God for *Consuelo*, our dishwasher.

So with hearts filled with gratitude and a tired baker, *hasta pronto*.
Egli

October 2, 2008, 9:24 p.m.
Day 172 on our road to recovery

Hey, it is me, Natalia.

It is now 10:24 p.m., Thursday night, and I am watching my favorite show, America's Funniest Home Videos. I watch this almost every night to get in a laugh or two before going to bed.

Two nights ago, I tried playing a game with my mom, and it was so funny because she could not last through the game. It is torture for her. Mommy doesn't know how to play any games. She can conduct extensive research, teach like no other teacher, be a super mommy and write papers, but can't play a game even if her life depended on it. Can you believe that? I am laughing out loud.

Tonight, I looked online for masks and dresses to wear for the masquerade fundraiser party that mommy's friends are planning for me. I want to look pretty, like a princess and dance again.

I can't wait! Well, I have to go, but thanks for always checking on me and writing to us.

Love ya!
Natalia

October 4, 2008, 12:34 a.m.
Día 174 en este largo y duro camino hacia nuestra recuperación

Queridos Guerrilleros,

My heart aches too much. I can't think in English anymore.

En esta madrugada desnudo mi alma contigo y te escribo en el idioma de mi corazón porque no puedo pensar en ingles. Las líneas fluyen como fluen mis lágrimas. Desde la oscuridad de nuestro hogar, en una noche iluminada por las estrellas de mi imaginación, me entrego una vez más a ti, mi Dios. Natalia duerme y mientras yo trato de entregar mis angustias y preocupaciones a ti, no puedo dejar de preocuparme y pedir piedad para mi niña. Ya basta de tanto sufrimiento y tanta tortura para una criatura tan inocente que solo sabe amar y sonreírle a la vida.

Cada media hora le tomo la temperatura como indicó su médico hace algunas horas y espero ese número mágico que indica si tenemos que salir corriendo hacia el hospital, o mantenernos en casa. Aunque su espíritu se mantiene contento y en su rostro hay una sonrisa cuando duerme, su hemoglobina sigue bajando, y su cuerpo pierde las fuerzas para combatir las bacterias que la siguen atacando.

En esta noche mis ojos no se secan y mi alma no entiende la lógica que ni las cabezas de los científicos entienden cómo una niña, al igual que miles de niños en este mundo dejaron de ser saludables para convertirse en niños gravemente enfermos de cáncer. Las razones y el por qué quizás nunca se sepan, lo único que se, es que duele en lo más profundo del alma cuando uno de esos niños enfermos es el tuyo, es la mía y solo me queda orar y creer que el amanecer traerá nuevas esperanzas. Solo me queda aferrarme a la esperanza que toda esta pesadilla que hoy yo vivo despierta pasará.

For those that can't read Spanish, don't worry. Natalia is stable and we are still at home checking her temperature every half hour. All of her counts were low this morning and she was put on two different antibiotics. She remains in good spirits. I just needed to undress my soul and write in its language, *Español*.

Con fe y esperanza,
Egli

October 5, 2008, 1:49 a.m.
Day 175 on our road to recovery

Dear Faithful Companions,

We got through another challenging twenty-four hours at home. Natalia continues to be in good spirits, and we are praying that there will be no hospitalization. She is responding well to both antibiotics. We will return to the hospital for a day full of tests on Monday, expecting nothing but the best results without space for doubts.

Thank you very much for your faithful prayers.

Egli

October 7, 2008, 1:10 p.m.
Day 177 on our road to recovery

Our Dearest Companions,

Our prayers have been heard and answered. Natalia's condition has improved. She is no longer neutropenic. Her white blood cell count went up as well as her hemoglobin, without the need for a blood transfusion or platelets.

She also gained one pound and three ounces. I don't know how she gained this pound; her head has been buried in a bucket vomiting constantly. Not questioning You today God, I'll take it. Thank You.

She is also taking steps on her own without the walker or the crutches. Gracias mi Dios, You never fail me, my dear God.

Con amor y agradecimiento,
Egli - Proud mommy of Natalia the Great, as she has been named by many.

October 13, 2008, 11:50 a.m.
Day 183 on our road to recovery

Hey, it is me, Natalia. I am here at the hospital and it really sucks being here. I don't feel like doing anything. I want to go home and be with my dog, Princess. In my mind, I am transporting myself home to bear with what is coming: more chemo.

I am excited about the masquerade fundraiser party at the end of the week; it gives me something to look forward to.

Natalia

October 16, 2008, 4:36 p.m.
Day 186 on our road to recovery

Dear Soldiers,

We are back in combat again for three consecutive weeks of chemo. Are you armed with faithful prayers? We are!

All week, I have been trying to find the words to write to you, and it has been difficult. This has been a rough week for Natalia. Her body has been weak. Her bones, limbs and joints have been in excruciating pain, and this has wiped out every ounce of energy from us.

Despite all the adversities, she continues to hope for better days to come. She started her week by having a mask painted on her face in preparation for the masquerade fundraiser dance that my awesome friends, "The Vermont Sisters" are having this Saturday. She has been preparing for this dance in physical therapy. She just pushed herself out of bed to go to physical therapy on the first floor. She wants to strengthen her leg.

Her goal is to be able to dance again and let me tell you that my baby girl is on her way. She is even walking a bit. Natalia is taking a few baby steps without her crutches. She is only allowed to put 50 pounds on her bionic leg, Will. I have to keep all four eyes on her because she has been putting her entire 105 pounds body weight on it.

We are both walking around with Goofy and Daisy duck stickers on our faces. They were earned in physical therapy today for a job well done. While she was exercising, I was napping, yet which was hard work for me.

The last time I saw my girl standing was six

months ago on April 14, at 6:22 p.m., which was the day she was diagnosed – the day our world became a dark cloud. That day, I thought I would never smile again, breathe again or dance again. This was the day I thought my heart stopped beating and I had stopped breathing, the day I knew I had to put my feelings aside and fight hard, stay focused and find the best medical care to save my daughter's life.

This was the day I thought my tears were never going to dry off my face, the day I thought I would never see the sunlight again. But, here we are almost two hundred days later, living in the sunshine, with some cloudy days, retaking baby steps, wanting to dance again, laughing more than ever, living more passionately, intentionally, hoping and dreaming so much more.

Natalia continues her fight to live a healthier life. We are back at Memorial Sloan Kettering for three consecutive weeks of treatments, but we were just sent home to get some sleep in our beds and return tomorrow at the crack of dawn. She was sent with an IV backpack for overnight hydration. I am the nurse on duty tonight. I will be waking her up for her medications and to check the pH levels.

Muchas gracias,
Egli – Proud mommy of little miss sunshine.

October 17, 2008, 10:15 p.m.
Day 187 on our road to recovery

Dear Companions,

Natalia is now resting after a long day at the hospital. She had to be hydrated most of the day and this afternoon she had to have a blood transfusion.

We were able to get medical clearance to attend the dance tomorrow. Natalia is thrilled! In her excitement, she played some music this evening before going to bed and asked me to practice dancing with her. She thought she had forgotten and I reminded her that dancing is like riding a bike; you don't forget.

"Dance with your soul girl," I said.

She is adjusting to her new leg and often questions what she can and cannot do. We feel God's presence when we look around and see that we are not going through this alone.

Thank you very much for your faithful prayers, they are being answered.

To my prayer group, soul sisters and friends, "The Vermont Sisters," thank you very much for celebrating Natalia's life in such a magnificent way. Your unconditional love and generosity are greatly appreciated.

Con fe, agradecimiento y esperanza,
Egli

October 20, 2008, 1:59 p.m.
Day 190 on our road to recovery

Dear Companions,

Just stopping quickly by the hospital's waiting room computer to let you know that the masquerade fundraiser dance was a great success. Thank you very much to "The Vermont Sisters" who organized the event, the contributors and all who attended.

Natalia and I had a great time; she even got to dance a bit. Thank you very much for having hearts of flesh and for being so generous to us during this challenging journey. Your kindness and generosity are greatly appreciated.

On a different note, we are moving forward with our treatments. As I write to you, Natalia is receiving chemo and we are expected to be here for the next two weeks. Natalia is already done with sixty percent of the treatments and we are staying focused on the finish line.

I took Natalia to physical therapy this morning and she was able to straighten her leg for the first time. Hooray! I think it was all the love and cheers from the party on Saturday that gave her the strength this morning.

My time is up on the computer; we can only use it for a limited amount of time because it is a public computer.

With much gratitude and love,
Egli

Natalia and Egli at a fundraiser hosted by the Vermont Sisters and their families; picture taken by Robert Flores.

October 23, 2008, 12:08 p.m.
Day 193 on our road to recovery

Dear Friends,

We are almost done with another week of treatments thank goodness! Natalia has been such a trooper. Despite all the adversities, she continues to strive for more and it seems like this week, she had a breath of new life breathed into her. I can't even keep up with her.

She has refused to give in, and each day, she has decided to get out of bed to feed her mind, body, soul and spirit with great things. She has been reading a lot, solving algebra problems, organizing and re-organizing her backpack and binders until late at night. She has even been talking about going to law school like her grandad, when she grows up, to become a lawyer and eventually, a judge.

By nature, Natalia has been independent and strong-willed. She left her bottle at fifteen months, her pacifier by eighteen and was potty-trained by twenty-two months. Natalia has been very analytical, opinionated and self-sufficient from an early age, but this week she has been on a roll. She has been pulling her IV pole everywhere and carrying her IV backpack when she is sent home. She has even been getting out of the room to be with other patients, playing, working, just being and enjoying life as it is at this time.

She has also been keeping track of her medications and documenting it on "mommy's medical chart." In other words, she has taken my job and it gives me great joy to see my daughter with so much strength and new life. All along, she has embraced this challenging situation with courage and has not resisted. It seems to me that she is ready to take over the world, so watch out! Natalia is coming to take over!

Thank you very much for all of your prayers, love and generous support. We are here today because we have been prayed for. Natalia and I are truly blessed to be surrounded by great people to get us through this challenging journey.

En paz y esperanza,
Egli

CHAPTER 12
FAITH AND COURAGE IN THE FACE OF ADVERSITY

Trust in the Lord with all your heart and lean not on your own understanding; in all your ways submit to him, and he will make your paths straight.
    - **Proverbs 3:5-6**

No hay rosas sin espinas.
    - **Esperanza Rising**

October 27, 2008, 12:04 a.m.
Day 197 on our road to recovery

Dear Faithful Companions,

It is past one in the morning and Natalia just managed to go to sleep. Usually, the night before we begin a new cycle, she gets a little anxious and can even start to taste the medicine. She is no longer innocent and naïve about the chemo process. Again, I have to find the strength I sometimes lack to support her. I lost track of what cycle we are on, what day it is and how many cycles we have left. These days I feel like I am on autopilot - pushing through and going through the motions. The only thing I know is that this is the last of three consecutive difficult weeks of seeing my baby being poked, probed and enduring the unimaginable.

We left the hospital Friday evening and made the best out of our weekend. Straight from the hospital, I took her to see the movie, High School Musical 3. This was our first outing since our lives changed last April. Going from the East Side to the West Side in a yellow cab was quite an adventure. We have developed a new sense of respect for people with disabilities. Thankfully, a very nice Indian driver in a minivan pulled over and helped us fold the wheelchair, put away the crutches and bags, and we were able to make it to the movies on time.

I enjoyed being driven across town for a change.

"Natalia, stop texting and enjoy the scenery."

"Mommy, you drive me all the time; it is time for you to enjoy the view and be driven," She replied.

After the movies, we ventured into Barnes and Noble like we used to on Friday nights when we lived in Brooklyn. Like old times, we went through all the aisles, picked up all the books and magazines that caught our eyes and started the process of elimination over a cup of tea and pastries at the Cafe. The first book she picked up surprised me, The Last Lecture by Randy Pausch. She was fascinated by his courageous story on the Oprah Winfrey show and decided to get the book. Professor Pausch gave this lecture around the time he was diagnosed in April and recently passed away from cancer. His story is pretty insightful and useful for our daily living. What can I say? My child has an old soul.

After a lovely evening at the movies and at Barnes and Noble, we took a cab back to the parking lot by the hospital and drove home. You may think it makes no sense to take a cab across town rather than take our own car, but parking can be very frustrating in New York City and we just wanted a stress-free evening. We had an amazing date!

The following day my friend Aissa got us tickets to the Big Apple Circus, and we went with my parents and my sister. It was Jenny's 24th birthday and we had a blast.

Natalia was sitting in her wheelchair among us with so many giggles and laughter that I almost forgot she was sick. I ended up with a sugar rush and a purple tongue from all the pink cotton candy and blue snow cones she made me eat.

The past forty-eight hours have been filled with laughter and family fun. We are hopeful that this joy can get us through this upcoming week. Natalia was even able to spend time with her little sister Ameerah and her dad when we left the circus. They both bring her much joy.

We are hoping for the best and embracing this new week,
Con paz y esperanza,
Egli

October 27, 2008, 8:35 p.m.
Day 197 on our road to recovery

Dear Faithful Companions,

Thanks for tuning in. Natalia's treatment had to be canceled for this week. Her blood counts are dropping, and this is scaring me. It doesn't sound good. Her white blood cells, red blood cells, and platelets are now low. The doctors have to wait for the counts to go up and in the meantime, Natalia has a lot of work to do in physical therapy. Treatments will hopefully resume next week.

We continue to move along; we are keeping our eyes fixed on healthier days and trusting that God's power get us through. There's no way around it.

Faithfully,
Egli

October 31, 2008, 10:23 a.m.
Day 201 on our road to recovery

Dear faithful companions,

This morning I write to you from our sanctuary, our peaceful new condo in Harlem. All is well and in divine order. Natalia is getting through this tough week. Her counts are low, but that is not stopping her from moving forward.

I have found myself moving at a faster pace too. This week, I made it a point to slow down a bit and be more attentive and reflective of my surroundings including myself. At times I don't want to allow my emotions to surface knowing that we are in the eye of the storm, but I know that the only way out is by going through.

Now that Natalia is back in her own room and I have my headquarters, I have more privacy and can allow myself to be. I have been going into my bathroom and literally submerging myself in a bubble filled tub and weeping.

In the midst of this storm, I also have to acknowledge the little blessings and the miracles we are experiencing. Natalia walked for the first time with full body weight. This makes me want to shout!

This miraculous event happened on Tuesday after we went to see Natalia's remarkable orthopedic surgeon. Natalia was only able to take a few steps on her own, but it felt as if she had just finished the New York City marathon as some of her school teachers will do in her honor this coming Sunday.

I almost missed this precious moment preoccupied and ranting to her surgeon about the appearance of the incision from the second surgery.

It healed well, but the vacuum used to extract the hematoma left a dent on her leg and this is beginning to annoy Natalia.

This week, Natalia also had a minor setback due to spasms on her hip, but the doctors say she will be walking on her own pretty soon. She is back to using both crutches, but in the next couple of weeks will only use one for balance. The wheelchair will only be used when she is on treatment or too tired.

God knows best, Dios sabe porque hace las cosas. We needed to catch up with our rest, and I desperately needed to regain my sanity. I felt I was beginning to lose my mind with 201 days in what it feels like a never-ending storm. I have allowed myself to put some things in perspective and see how far we have come, how blessed and loved we are.

I have said it before and here I go again, "I have always been a better giver than a receiver." I am really struggling to accept. It is not pride; giving of myself has always been easier for me and being on the receiving end at this point in my life has forced me to grow. I am learning to extend my hands, open a little crack in my heart to receive and be grateful. I feel like I am being broken open and made whole. This is, by far, one of the hardest lessons I have had to learn lately. This situation has made me so vulnerable.

From the continuous length of this entry, you can tell I am home alone this morning. Natalia is in Brooklyn at her Nana's house baking pumpkin cupcakes. I'll pick her up later to go trick or treating and into the Halloween parade in Park Slope. Before then, I am going to go for a brisk walk at Central Park. Yes, I am running/walking in solidarity with all who are running to find a cure for cancer, especially those honoring my daughter, Carlos and Chris, from Natalia's school, The Young Women's Leadership School (TYWLS). I am now up to five miles a day. They have inspired me to shake things off and stop suppressing my feelings.

I dream of the day this world can be cancer free, and I hope one day I can run the marathon too. In the meantime, I will continue running for Natalia and me, and we will cheer for all the runners on Sunday.

One step at a time, one breath at a time, one mile at a time.

Salud,
Egli

November 3, 2008, 1:52 p.m.
Day 204 on our road to recovery

Dearest Companions,

    Thank you very much for running this marathon with us and cheering us on this journey. Yesterday was the New York City Marathon. We were able to see the runners from 5th Avenue, just a block away from home. I was amazed to see Carlos, Natalia's former basketball coach and dean at The Young Women's Leadership School running with a picture of Natalia laminated on the back of his shirt. I was so touched by this kind gesture that I ran along his side for over a block thanking him. As tired as he was when he got to Harlem, he kept shouting, "Tell Natalia she is going to make it." I truly believe this; we are walking by faith and not by sight. I need to continually tell myself to get over my fearful thinking and transform my mind. She will get through this.

    I am writing to you from home again today. We just got here from the hospital and the oncology team is trying an experiment on Natalia this week. She was sent home with chemo infusion until Thursday. I got tons of instructions on what to expect and how to monitor her. The chemo she is on this week is called Doxorubicin and is usually given in conjunction with Cisplatin, but she has completed that one and now only gets Doxorubicin. I am familiar with the side effects and how to operate the pump that allows the red cocktail, Doxorubicin, to enter. This one is brutal; it scares me, however, we can only hope for the best.

    In the event she gets too sick, and I can't handle it here, I have been instructed to rush her to the hospital. I am feeling pretty confident about being able to do this, but please continue to pray for us. Natalia needs strength and lots of prayers to get through this rough patch. During moments like these, I miss living with my parents and sister, but I am glad we are only a hop and a skip away from Memorial Sloan Kettering and not far from my parents in Brooklyn. We are doing our best to stay away from there this week.

I never expected to celebrate my birthday under these circumstances. I am so thankful for my health, and for the many birthday texts, phone calls and emails received since midnight. Mami came to visit today. She showed up at my door with a cupcake and a lit candle singing happy birthday. She is missing 36 candles; today is my 37th birthday. My only birthday and life-long wish is for my daughter's health to be restored. Things are hectic around here and I expect them to be for the rest of the week. Our reality is very different, but I am already envisioning better days. My daughter is on her way to recovery and I am having a great birthday.

Besitos y abrazos from the birthday girl,
Egli

November 4, 2008, 2:46 p.m.
Day 205 on our road to recovery

Dear Faithful Companions,

All is well and in divine order. We continue to walk by faith and not by sight, although Natalia is looking pretty good these days. She had a good night sleep and is responding well to the chemo IV at home. Things seem to be under control here and she is thrilled about the presidential elections. She loves Barack Obama and has been campaigning for him at the hospital.

There were some difficulties while voting in Harlem today. Although Natalia is only thirteen, she wanted to witness the voting process with me, so she asked me to help her get in her wheelchair. With her chemo backpack and all, she made me take a ride to my old voting site in Brooklyn. I hope that when she is older, she exercises this right with this much conviction. I registered to vote in Harlem when we first moved, but the system is showing that I still reside in Brooklyn. This was a good excuse to visit my parents. We picked up my mom and while I voted she stayed with Natalia in the car. Mami became a U.S. citizen a few years back and Natalia is thrilled to have another person vote for Obama. Mami doesn't need any convincing; she loves him just as much. Nothing was going to stop us from voting today; our nation is in as much need of healing as we are. Natalia is laying by my side, telling me to make sure I tell all of our faithful readers to get out and vote. She says, "Vote for a change, vote for Barack Obama." Do I have a future politician here? I doubt it; she just loves Mr. Obama!

On a different note, I had an amazing birthday.

I love all the emerging changes.

Exercise your right. Vote!
Egli

Natalia and Egli campaigning for President Obama on the hospital's pediatric floor en route to getting chemotherapy.

November 6, 2008, 1:36 p.m.
Day 207 on our road to recovery

Hey, it is me, Natalia,

I just got home from the hospital. The doctors unhooked my port and gave me a shot for my electrolytes to go up. This week, they tried a new experiment on me. I was allowed to go home with the chemo instead of going to the hospital every morning. I enjoy being in the comfort of our own home. I think it is better than always being in the hospital all day.

I was so excited to watch the elections at home. I have never been this thrilled about politics and I am so happy that Mr. Barack Obama won. This is the second time in my lifetime that I get so involved in the elections. I believe I was in the second grade during the last election and my teacher got us really into it. I am older now and I have chosen to get involved even if I can't vote. I really like President Obama, his wife Michelle and his daughters Sasha and Malia. It felt like New Year's Eve all over again in Harlem when it was announced on television past midnight that he won.

It felt as if we were in Times Square with people shouting and screaming. Mommy and I were shouting too. It was way past my bedtime, but she let me stay up to celebrate this victory. She was jumping with joy, and we hugged as if we were the ones moving into the White House tomorrow. Our trip to Brooklyn to vote was so worth it. The new presidential election has mommy celebrating every day. I have to say she has turned into a gourmet chef this week. She cooked a lot. I have not been puking much and gained some weight. I am now 113 pounds.

I am looking forward to having some time off to regain my strength. I believe I have about a week or two off treatments.

Before we left the hospital today, I had to wait until my chemo IV was finished. Mommy attempted to distract me by trying to play pool with me in the recreation room. She is quite a character and I am up for her tricks. She forgets that she can't play any games.

Well, *adios* for now. Smooches.
Natalia

Egli Colón Stephens, Ed.D.

November 13, 2008, 12:50 a.m.
Day 214 on our road to recovery

Dear Companions, *Mis Queridos Compañeros en la Lucha*,

It is almost 2:00 a.m., Natalia is asleep and I should go to bed too. We have regressed to when she was a baby. I should sleep when she sleeps, but I had to give you a brief update on her.

We were given two weeks off chemo to let her body recover from last week's treatment, but it really doesn't feel like time off. Is this a trick? We started the week well, her blood counts were up, she was walking and going up and down a set of stairs with her crutches in physical therapy at the hospital. She even visited her school at the beginning of the week.

Unfortunately, she has been in bed since then with brutal side effects from last week's chemo and what I think is a strained muscle on "Will." I am beginning to question if she is ready to walk on both legs with full body weight. Every time she tries to walk with full weight bearing, 113 pounds, she ends up in bed with excruciating pain for two to three days. We are expected at the hospital in the morning to check her platelets and I will discuss the problem we are having with the leg. I guess her leg has to adjust to the prosthesis. I can't speculate or only make guesses when it comes to my daughter's wellbeing; I need concrete answers.

On a different note, Natalia is now reading Esperanza Rising along with everyone in her 8th grade English class. She needs to distract herself from the pain and discomfort. Here's a quote that caught our attention last night as we were reading to one another; it reminds me of her:

"We are like the Phoenix, said *abuelita*, rising again, with a new life ahead of us."

This too shall pass and she, we, will rise again with new life like the Phoenix.

Always rising,
Egli and Nat

November 13, 2008, 10:39 p.m.
Day 214 on our road to recovery

Beloved, *Queridos y Queridas*,

Natalia was on the list for a possible blood and platelet transfusion today, but guess what? Our God is so awesome that this was not necessary. Thank Jesus for having mercy on my little girl. Thank You for blessing us with Your grace. Her blood counts are still holding up. Nurse Paulette said, "We can't believe it! What are you giving her? What are you doing? You need to share it with the world!"

We responded, "Prayers, lots of prayers and faith. When we are too tired to pray for ourselves, we have an entire army praying for us."

Faith is all we have. We are praying and believing that Natalia will rise again. I also truly believe that my good cooking has healing powers too, it revives the dead like my friends often say. In addition to not being able to play any games, I can't follow a recipe to save my life. So I add good homemade *sazón* and lots of *amor* to everything.

Her leg pain seems to be getting better, but it could be the strong muscle relaxer she was prescribed. I am anxious and very concerned about this. My motherly intuition never fails and something just doesn't seem right. I am praying that I am wrong on this one, sweet Jesus. Please let me be wrong, but I am going to get to the bottom of what is causing this damn pain.

I asked them to examine her leg and run some X-rays. Her surgeon is away for the week, but the chief resident who saw the X-rays says that nothing seems abnormal. Further tests will be done next week. In the meantime, she was told to stay off the leg.

We are counting our blessings. We are also rejoicing in the chief resident's words, "Nothing seems abnormal" and the fact that she did not need a blood and platelet transfusion today.

Thank You God for scratching Natalia's name off that transfusion list. You are still in the business of making miracles. You are all we have. Thanks! I am winking and giving You thumbs up.

I have to go now; Natalia is rushing me to get off the computer so that I can help her create a picture book with all of her paintings from when she was younger. Putting on my crafty mom-hat now. I hope this is a way of de-cluttering some drawers. She wants me to get rid of all of her paintings and papers with chicken scratch handwriting, *garabatos* from Pre-K to date by taking pictures of them and compiling them all into a picture book. She doesn't understand that these are treasures to a parent.

Adelante, siempre adelante,
Egli

November 18, 2008, 2:56 a.m.
Day 219 on our road to recovery

Dear faithful companions,

Natalia and I had an eventful weekend. On Friday night, we went to a fashion show organized by our dear friend, Matthew Quiñones, at the Church for All People in Brooklyn. We had a great time. All the proceeds of the fashion show were kindly gifted to us for our living expenses since I have not been able to return to work. Natalia's dad provides health insurance and child support, but I had to take out a personal loan to cover the rest of our expenses.

We are so touched by the generosity and thoughtfulness of our friends. They just want me to focus on taking care of Natalia and not worry about anything. I will be forever grateful to "Mashew," like Natalia used to call him when she was little.

Many thanks to all the models and all those who volunteered their time, gifts and talents to make this a great event. ¡Muchas gracias!

On a different note, Saturday, the day after the show, Natalia tried to rest most of the day, but her leg was still hurting. The muscle relaxer is no longer helping, and she needs something stronger. I am getting really worried. I did not sleep and kept walking back and forth at our home, wondering what was now wrong with Will. Something doesn't feel right. I did not want to alarm her by calling an ambulance, but as soon as daylight broke, we were out the door. I took her to Urgent Care again at Memorial Sloan Kettering.

The pain in her leg has not subsided. New X-rays were taken, but they do not reveal any abnormalities. The doctors said the prosthesis looks fine. Thank God! I must admit that all kinds of scary thoughts have taken over my mind during these past few sleepless nights. There is something about the midnight hours that can drive anyone in our situation insane. I can't help it; I am only human.

Could the leg be infected? Could there be another tumor growing? These thoughts invade my mind like a plague once I put Natalia to sleep. I stare at the ceiling, get out of bed, walk around, get on my knees, get up again, as my thoughts run a thousand miles an hour, until I finally throw myself in bed and fall asleep out of exhaustion. I surrender to You, sweet Jesus and ask You to get us through this. I tell myself that I need to trust what I am being told.

"Everything is fine in there."

"Unfortunately this pain is expected as part of the rehabilitation process. The bones that are attached to the prosthesis need to get used to it and the leg will hurt." The head of the orthopedic department who examined her said.

"Natalia had major leg reconstruction, and the healing process is slow and painful." He continued.

I am having a hard time accepting this. My daughter is undergoing too much. It is hard to be patient when your kid is in pain. I feel helpless. This is the worst pain I have ever seen Natalia in since she got out of the operating room. Today, she is responding better to the painkillers, but just like myself, she is afraid of taking pain medication in fear of becoming dependent on it.

Tomorrow, we return to physical therapy and must continue rehab through the pain. I don't know how much longer we are going to be able to keep pushing through. I am growing weary having a hard time believing that all this pain and anguish is going to return my daughter to health. I feel helpless. I want to run away with her. It has been frustrating to see her in so much pain and not being able to do anything for her but hold her hand, pray and let her lean on me. I don't want to lie, but it is not getting any better.

It is now 3:30 a.m. and she just let go of my hand. I am going to get some rest before she notices I am not lying next to her.

Gladys, Maggie and Heather, thanks for the visit today and for bringing us dinner. Thank You God, for continuing to place earth angels in our lives. Even during our darkest hour, I am turning to You. I cannot fail to see the goodness that surrounds us.

Bye for now,
Egli

November 21, 2008, 1:52 a.m.
Day 222 on our road to recovery

Dear faithful companions,

With an attitude of gratitude, we would like to thank you all for your love and support and wish you a very Happy Thanksgiving next week.

Natalia is getting through the week, one step and one breath at a time.

We met with the chief of orthopedics today and he does not have an explanation for the recurrent pain on Natalia's leg. It is frustrating not to have concrete answers, but this situation has been another lesson on acceptance for us, although we are having some difficulties getting it. It is what it is and for that, we give thanks.

Natalia is in great spirits, embracing her discomfort with grace, courage and serenity. She is doing better than I am; I want to pull my little hairs out.

We are now on a break from chemo until December 1st, so we are taking a few mental days off too.

With an attitude of gratitude for what is,
Egli and Natalia

December 1, 2008, 1:57 p.m.
Day 232 on our road to recovery

Dear Companions,

    We hope you all had an enjoyable Thanksgiving. Indeed, there is so much to be thankful for. Our Thanksgiving was great. I was not kidding when I said I wanted to take my daughter away from all that reminded her of our current reality.

    We escaped from New York City with my mom and Jenny to a magical place for a few days. Natalia was in desperate need of a distraction and some fun. We got the okay from her care team to go.

    God's earth angels are everywhere. I would not have been able to pull this trip off without the generosity of our loved ones. Thanks to my dear friend from college, Maria who let us use her timeshare and to Natalia's uncle, David, who got us into the Disney parks. We spent four magical days filled with laughter, creating great memories.

    Although Natalia still has some discomfort on her leg, she was able to get on all the scary rides and even tricked my mom into getting on them with us. There's nothing Mami would not do to see her girl smile, even get on the Free Fall ride. She had no clue that the elevator-looking-thing was going to drop us from so high up. The look on her face was priceless. Natalia was hysterical and Mami almost died.

    We got back on Wednesday night and spent these past few days enjoying our family's warmth at my parents.

    We are now at the hospital for three consecutive weeks of chemotherapy. To our surprise, we were informed this morning that the end of this agony is near. If all goes as expected, Natalia's chemo treatments will end at the end of January. Hooray for our warrior! We will then begin an intense rehabilitation process to get her leg strong again and back on her feet.

As we approach this season of hope, expectation, and celebration, I can't ask for a better gift than to have my daughter's health restored, and it seems we are on our way.

Thanks and praise be to God, thanks for being my co-parent, especially during the dark hours of the night.

With an attitude of gratitude, cheers, and *esperanza*,
Egli

Natalia's much needed getaway to Disney World during treatment and with the broken leg, Will.

December 10, 2008, 9:25 a.m.
Day 241 on our road to recovery

Dear Companions,

We have encountered some bumps on the way, and things have gotten more challenging. Please continue to pray for Natalia's healing, strength, and wisdom for the physicians who care for her.

We need the endurance to overcome this storm.

I need you to pray for me, for us. I am having a hard time picking myself up to pray for Natalia and me.

In hope and faith,
Egli

December 17, 2008, 1:11 p.m.
Day 248 on our road to recovery

Dear companions,

Many thanks for your prayers, wishes for joy, healing, love and strength. They are sustaining us. We are on our third week of consecutive chemotherapy and Natalia is still going strong. My apologies for not keeping you as updated as I should, but things have been beyond challenging lately and I am feeling overwhelmed and defeated.

On December 3rd, we saw Natalia's orthopedic surgeon who had been away for almost a month. She confirmed my instinct that there was something wrong with Natalia's leg. The leg broke and the prosthesis too. I literally want to hide under a rock. No wonder I kept feeling so uneasy, a mother's instinct never fails.

Yes, you are reading correctly. The leg that Natalia was operated on twice this summer and got the 18-inch titanium prosthesis inserted with a full knee replacement is broken.

For those of you reading this for the first time, please breathe. We are also trying to wrap our minds around it. The grace of God is sustaining us. We have come too far and He is not going to leave us now. This, I know for sure.

Again, I apologize for not letting you know sooner, but Natalia's Nana was out of the country, and we did not want to upset her with this horrible news while she was back home in Barbados. Natalia has taken this setback with tremendous courage. On the other hand, I am not. I kept asking the doctor the same question hoping to hear a different answer. I could not believe what I was hearing. This cannot be happening to us, "We are good people. We are women of faith." I said.

I am glad I know better than to blame God for this. I don't think I will ever understand why this is happening to us, perhaps it is not for me to understand, but all I know is that it hurts. It hurts me deeply to see my daughter hurting.

There was nothing she or we did wrong to break the leg, the orthopedic surgeon said. "Unfortunately, her bones have become very brittle as a result of so much chemotherapy, but it was necessary to save her life."

Natalia has made a bold decision again, and I am honoring it. She decided to complete her chemo treatments before going back to the operating room to reconstruct the leg. Her leg is now on a brace again and she has been given stronger medicine to manage the pain. Hopefully, by mid-January, we should be done with the treatments and can begin to plan when Natalia can go back to the operating room. As I have written here before, Natalia has been in discomfort for a while.

Since the day Natalia put full body weight on her leg, October 28, she has been complaining of pain in her leg. I trusted my maternal instinct, I knew something was not right and I took her to Urgent Care twice. She was even seen by the chief of orthopedic surgery, and apparently, none of the X-rays revealed any fractures or infection of the prosthesis. Everything was supposedly fine and we were told that the pain was muscular because of the major leg reconstruction (as if we did not know it), and it was going to take a while to heal. I can go on and on with the different scenarios we were given, but it is not worth it now. I can't deplete myself.

This setback is very upsetting for us and we

have cried our eyes out, but we are at peace now. We feel this went undiagnosed for so long. Natalia endured so much pain and so much could have been done differently, but at the end of the day, we have no time or energy to waste in all of the "what-ifs?"

Her surgeon realized that maybe in the future, they need to keep female patients with femur Osteosarcoma off the leg until they complete their chemo treatments. Apparently, their bones become like women with osteoporosis, very weak. I wish this realization had been made before my daughter's leg broke.

We can sit here and lament all we want and point fingers, but we are almost at the finish line and with a leg to fix. We are embracing this new challenge with serenity, courage and surrendering each day. We continue to move forward joyfully, embracing our dreams and hopes for firm steps again. This too shall pass.

Paz,
Egli

December 25, 2008, 11:30 p.m.
Day 256 on our road to recovery

Dear Companions,

Love was created at Christmas time with the birth of Jesus, and throughout the day, I have been reminded that even in our moments of darkness, there's a glimpse of light. There's always something or someone to be thankful for and to remind us that we are loved. We are truly surrounded by pure and genuine love. Natalia radiates love which strengthens us to keep pushing forward every day.

All is in divine order in our lives; we are taking things in strides. This is a different kind of Christmas, one we could have never imagined, but our hearts are full. Although I feel helpless, we have consciously chosen to remain in a state of gratitude. As humans, yes, we wish our lives had not been struck by cancer, but the prayer of acceptance comes to mind, and all I can pray for is courage. We need the courage to go on because we have no control over this situation. I pray that I can embody courage and model it for my daughter. I pray that I may continue to surrender to God's plan for our lives. I don't mean surrender as in giving up; I am talking about the kind of surrender when you lift your arms and only ask God to hold you, embrace you, and help you carry your burdens.

Natalia continues to make progress each day. The leg is still broken and as hard as it is, I respect her decision to keep it broken until she is done with all the chemo treatments. She knows her body best and has shown me a great deal of autonomy and maturity during this ordeal. She knows her limits and wants to focus on one thing at the time.

Right now, she is focusing her strength on finishing her treatments before going back to the operating room to repair her leg. I am struggling to accept this decision, but this was an educated decision that she made with her physicians.

"Jesus, I wonder if Mary hurt this much when she saw You being crucified?"
I feel helpless.

For the gift of Natalia's relentless spirit and so much more, I give You thanks, my Magnificent God.

Merry Christmas and may the love of this season bring warmth and comfort to your hearts.

Con amor,
Egli

CHAPTER 13
LIKE THE PHOENIX WE RISE

Do not gloat over me, my enemy! Though I have fallen, I will rise. Though I sit in darkness, the Lord will be my light.
        - Micah 7:8

The phoenix hope can wing her way through the desert skies, and still defying fortune's spite; revive from ashes and rise.
        - Miguel de Cervantes Saavedra

January 5, 2009, 10:15 p.m.
Day 267 on our road to recovery (Day 1 of our last two weeks of chemo)

Dear Faithful Companions,

Happy New Year to all! These words now have a new and more profound meaning to me. As I repeat them, I am more conscious of what I wish you and sincerely mean these words and desire them for myself too. In addition to happiness, I also wish you good health. I will also say, "Have a Happy and Healthy New Year!"

Health brings us happiness, and although I have always appreciated and taken good care of my health, it took this situation to appreciate it even more. Health is wealth.

During this battle with cancer, I have realized that our most valuable asset is our health. When we have a healthy mind, body, soul and spirit, we are perfectly aligned with the divine and from there, everything else flows.

May this New Year, 2009, bring us health, peace, balance, happy endings, new beginnings and fulfillment of dreams.

We are almost at the finish line and can see the light at the end of the tunnel. We feel like we are dragging, or perhaps, crawling to the finish line. Sometimes, the last stretch of a marathon can be hardest. This is a challenging stretch for my girl.

We are back at the hospital for our last two weeks of treatments. Today, as the chemo IV entered her veins again, the brutal side effects invaded her body. I immediately noticed her fighting to stay strong and not be defeated.

Let us unite in prayer and send fortitude to

strengthen my sweet girl. Today, she was in more pain than usual and became anxious as doubts crossed her mind.

"Mommy, I am afraid of not making it. I am tired. I don't want to do this anymore," She whispered as I was gently rubbing her head.

Her body is tired and her leg is broken, but I know that deep inside, her spirit remains filled with hope. These words come from frustration as the chemo instantly robs her of her strength.

I can taste the victory. I need to remain strong for the both of us. We continue to walk by faith and not by sight. I rebuke her words of defeat and desperation and replace them with renewed strength, endurance and determination. Our Lord got us this far and will not abandon us now. This, I know for sure.

On this eve of the Epiphany, I re-gift my heart and life to You Lord, in return for my daughter's health. I don't want to bargain with You, but I am desperate. Hear my plea. You are all we have got, and I need You to turn things around for us. Please strengthen her body, renew her mind, heal her spirit and help us end this battle strong. I know You can and will do this for us. Amen.

In God's grace,
Egli - Proud mommy of a true warrior.

January 7, 2009, 3:30 p.m.
Day 267 on our road to recovery

My Dearest Soldiers,

We are still in combat, but I am glad our journey is almost coming to an end. Gracias a Dios we only have two more weeks of treatments, though these seem to be the hardest because we are physically and mentally drained.

Natalia is getting through this grueling week, one breath and one piggyback ride at a time. Yes, piggyback rides are back! At times I have had to carry my 5'10", 108 pounds baby. A mother needs to do whatever she needs to do for her child and we are determined to make it to the finish line together, even if I have to carry her on my back. I am never letting go.

Her frail body and bones have been in excruciating pain this week. It is unlike Natalia, to not receive her lessons or leave the hospital room to play with other kids in the playroom. She has been sedated most of the week, but yesterday, she woke up for a few minutes and smiled at me. Moments like these are priceless.

She turned my world around with a smile when I showed her pictures on the computer of the Three Kings Day parade held in Harlem at El Museo del Barrio. She remembered the time she fed carrots to the camels during a parade I took my students to in 2006. Seeing these pictures brought her sweet memories.

Last night, she had sushi and some left-over paella from Sunday's dinner. Today, she was more alert and slowly regained some energy. She ate a beef burrito and some more left-over paella for dinner.

My mom is spending the night to relieve me from the night shift. I am looking forward to having some uninterrupted sleep tonight. Mami will play nurse, document Natalia's progress on the health chart, measure the pH level in her urine and give her the medications.

I was beginning to lose my sanity but thank goodness for a mom like mine. The way I mother Natalia, is the way she has mothered me. She has been my greatest teacher.

Again, thank you for carrying us through our darkest hours. Your prayers, love and support sustain us. When I doubt God's presence in all of this, I see Him in the compassionate, kind-hearted and generous people that surround us.

In faith,
Egli - Proud mommy of the bravest warrior I know. "Keep leading the way Natalia, mommy will follow your lead." *Te amo.*

January 9, 2009, 12:38 p.m.
Day 269 on our road to recovery

Dear Faithful Companions,

We did it! We have one more week of chemo to go. Natalia and I are at home. She is resting and reading Twilight while I am putting away Christmas decorations and putting out the tree. It is past Three Kings Day and Christmas is officially over. This was our first Christmas in our new condo and it was spectacular, especially considering our circumstances.

We were given today off from the hospital since all of her tests results were fine. It is exciting to be reaching the finish line, but at the same time sad when others who have been fighting this battle with all their might, will not make it. It saddens my heart deeply, but I have to mentally put blinders on and remind my daughter that our story will have a different ending.

There was a lot of chaos at the hospital yesterday, Shaquana, a patient we know, went into cardiac arrest next to Natalia's room at the Pediatric Cancer Clinic. The rooms are small here and the dividing panels do not go up to the ceiling. Therefore, we can hear everything that goes on in the next room and only imagine what is going on. We saw the nurses rushing into the room and could hear the chaos so vividly. The family was told to wait outside while they cried and ran up and down the hallways in desperation, hoping for the best. I closed the curtain to keep Natalia from seeing the madness in the hallway but felt terrified, however, remaining as calm as possible to keep her from panicking.

This teen girl danced with us at the prom last

June. We saw her a couple of times after that at the clinic and now, she is dead. It freaked me out and I did not want to ask questions or let Natalia get too involved. We stayed in our room as I desperately waited for the last drop of hydration IV to finish. I bundled Natalia up, sat her on her wheelchair and rushed out of the hospital faster than a bullet. I have never pushed Natalia's wheelchair as fast as I did yesterday.

We were all saddened. The staff held back tears and were stunned at how fast Shaquana was gone.

Although this breaks my heart, I need to protect my little girl's heart and mind. We have coped with our situation by being compassionate of others, but we learned to protect our space by keeping away from any more tragic situations. As much as I enjoy socializing with the other parents on the floor, whenever I hear or see pessimistic behavior, I excuse myself and leave. I don't allow anyone to talk about death or make projections on my daughter based on what has happened to other patients with similar conditions, reminding them that not all cancers are the same or Osteosarcomas are alike.

As we come near the end of our journey, death seems to be lingering on the pediatric floor. I have witnessed children who fought hard alongside us, but did not make it to the finish line. As difficult as it is to stay focused under these circumstances, all we can do is pray. This evening as we were leaving the hospital, we were informed of another patient's death.

Patrick was a fine young man who was a big fan of the Phillies. He lost his battle with cancer on Saturday. The news was a big shock for us because he seemed to be making progress. His mother is very angry, and cannot explain how his CAT scans changed so drastically from one month to the next.

My mom and I were so overwhelmed that we rushed Natalia out of the hospital again for some fresh air to clear our minds and our heavy hearts. We felt suffocated as if a gray cloud had come over our sunny and bright pediatric floor. It is impossible not to feel someone else's pain and loss, but we must remain focused on our journey. I don't want to think about the "what-ifs," but at times I do, and so does Natalia. We have begun to talk about things like her future and plan her sweet sixteen birthday party. She talks about her wedding day and loves to talk about the kind of grandmother she will one day be. Oh, Lord, help me! Natalia plans to live a very long life, and those are my hopes and dreams for her too. I need to believe deeply and have faith that my daughter is cured regardless of what we see around us.

I once read somewhere that faith believes without doubts and I believe that my daughter will live a long, healthy and peaceful life. So today Lord, I surrender all of my fears, doubts, and trust that when the sun rises tomorrow, I will have a renewed spirit. Amen.

In faith,
Egli - Proud mommy of a faith-filled warrior.

January 12, 2009, 1:13 p.m.
Day 272 on our road to recovery

Dear Faithful Companions,

We are back at the hospital for our final round of chemo. Hooray! I have been waiting a very long time to say this and I will say it one more time: This is our last round of chemo! Natalia has been going non-stop since last April and we are feeling victorious to be reaching the finish line. We barely slept last night in excitement and anticipation of the week ahead. We had our bags ready, clothes out, shoes, crutches and the wheelchair lined up by the door ready to go. When the alarm clock went off this morning at 6:30 a.m., we did not press the snooze button. We were prepared to go and embrace the day with a huge smile. We said "Let's do this!" to each other as we left the house.

Driving east on 116th street and approaching the FDR drive, the sun was rising and caressing us with its warmth. Life was smiling at us again. Today, more than ever before, God spoke to us through that sunrise.

Natalia's blood tests came back great and we were started by 11:00 a.m. As I write to you now, the last one thousand milligrams of Methotrexate chemotherapy IV is going in. She hates to see the bright yellow fluid entering her veins and asked me to put a huge white sheet over the IV pole which makes it look like a ghost.

I am finding myself quiet, though mentally talking to the IV pole. Praying and begging this medication to kill any possible cancerous cells that may still exist in her body and to prevent them from ever returning. I can't ever imagine us doing this again. Natalia is getting her school lesson as she lays in bed receiving her medications with her arm extended resting on a pillow. They are discussing an article about top teens of the 20th Century like Anne Frank, Mozart and many others. I believe my warrior is one of the top teens of this century. My daughter rocks! She exceeded my expectations. I don't think I would have endured this misery if I was in her place. She is resilient, brave, courageous and awesome; I hope she never forgets that.

Life and our existence have become so simple and basic this past year despite our battle. Natalia and I have become so much more patient and compassionate towards each other. We no longer find ourselves sweating the small stuff. We are most grateful and appreciative of the simple things we took for granted, such as waking up in the right frame of mind each morning, breathing, eating and simply being.

Her appetite returned this morning. She asked me to get some sushi for lunch and ate half of what she was served. She is in great spirits and already making a list of the first five things she wants to do when she is done with treatments. I don't even want to think of our next journey to repair the broken leg. We are staying present as we celebrate and taste this victory. God is good all the time, and all the time, God is good. Oh, victory tastes so good!

Saboreando nuestra victoria,
Egli - Proud mommy of Natalia the brave!

January 13, 2009, 10:14 a.m.
Day 273 on our road to recovery

HEY, HEY, HEY, EVERYONE!

First of all, I want to say thanks to my family and friends for helping me reach my last step. This is my last chemo treatment and I can't begin to tell you how happy I am. I am almost done!

I would not have made it this far without the love and support of my family and friends, but more importantly, the help of God. Thank you from the bottom of my heart.

I have truly been blessed during my most challenging time and it is important that I bless someone else and pay it forward. There is an eleven-year-old girl who is starting the same process I went through and she has lots of questions. She is an Osteosarcoma patient from Perú named Mariana. She came into my room today and asked if she could ask me a few questions. It feels great to be able to help someone else and maybe, I can make her journey a little easier. Her surgery is at the end of the month and I would like to ask you to please pray for her because I know prayers are powerful. She asked to see my scar and wanted to know if I was in pain when I woke up from surgery. Before she left for her room, she said, "You are my hero." I did not know what to say; I gave this battle my all. I wanted to live and had to do all that I could. I hope I can continue to help others on this journey.

Love,
Natalia
*PEACE*LOVE*STRENGTH

January 14, 2009, 10:21 p.m.
Day 274 on our road to recovery

Dear Faithful Companions,

Tonight, I sit here in complete awe and admiration as I watch Natalia, full of life and dreams to fulfill. She is ready to end this part of her journey and move on with her life. Her strength, maturity, and determination have been remarkable.

The end is near, and we are hoping that tomorrow is our last day of hydration to flush the chemo out of her body. For the past two nights, she has been coming home with the popular IV backpack and we can't wait to kiss it goodbye forever.

The side effects have been brutal as usual, but just knowing that the end is near has given her the strength to keep pushing forward. As she pukes her heart out, she reminds me, "This is it mommy, no more chemo for me," and I assure her that she is right, "This is it!"

Tomorrow, we have another day of hydration at the hospital and lots of scans to confirm that she is cancer free and that this journey has been worth it. I am feeling so many mixed emotions and I bring them before God because He already knows my mind and my heavy heart. I am afraid of tomorrow's tests, but I continue to surrender, believe, breathe, give thanks, let go and embrace life. We are ready for new beginnings.

We are expecting to finalize the details of operation number three to repair the broken leg next week. As we end one journey, we begin another. In the meantime, she has a lot of recovering to do. We need to get her body
stronger before she goes into the operating room.

Thanks again for making it to the finish line

with us. This is not just our victory; it is your victory as well. It takes a community to raise a child, and you have done this with us. Your prayers, love, support, words of encouragement and generosity has brought us this far.

In faith,
Egli - Proud mommy of Natalia - the brave one.

**January 15, 2009, 7:55 p.m.
Day 275 on our road to recovery**

Dear Faithful Companions,

Natalia made it to the finish line. Praise God! This part of the journey is over. I am simply overwhelmed with unimaginable peace. I have nothing else to say.

Thank You God for being my strength.

With love, faith and gratitude,
Egli

February 2, 2009, 1:37 p.m.
Day 293 on our road to recovery

Dear Friends,

It is Natalia writing to you. It has been a while since I last wrote. I am doing well, resting, mending and preparing for my third and hopefully, the last surgery. Last week was our first full week at home and I did not get poked or probed, thank God. I am doing really well, already growing some peach fuzz on my head and gaining some weight.

Yesterday, The Vermont sisters (mommy's prayer warriors) and five of their daughters came over to celebrate the end of my battle. It was a Thanksgiving feast in February. We had a delicious banquet! It was so much fun to be with our friends, celebrating and giving thanks. Every day, I thank God for my life, my health, family, and friends.

Today, I woke up to my dog, Princess, being reprimanded by mommy because she did something bad. Even if she gets in trouble, she gives me puppy dog eyes, and in a few minutes, I am tempted to like her again. My doggy gives me so much joy when I come home from the hospital after a long day of treatment. She can put a smile on my face regardless of how hard my day has been.

Today, I also woke up to the news that my surgery is coming soon. I knew it was coming but did not know when mommy was going to book it. I tried to block it out of my mind and deal with things day by day. Mommy just came into my room and told me she booked it for Thursday, February 19th. I am excited and a little anxious at the same time. I have mixed emotions, but I know God is going to be in the operating room with me and helping the orthopedic surgeon and her team reconstruct my leg again. I am not questioning why these things happened to me; I am saving my energy to fight and overcome the obstacles.

Thank you for sticking by my side and giving me the strength to make it to the finish line. All of my scans are back, and I am officially cancer free. I am officially a cancer survivor! If I can do this, I can do anything I set my mind on. YAYYYYYYYYYYY!!!!!!!

With love and gratitude,
Natalia
Officially a cancer survivor!

Natalia is cancer free after multiple surgeries and many rounds of chemotherapy.

February 19, 2009, 3:04 p.m.
Day 310 on our road to recovery

Dear Friends and Family,
    I am writing on behalf of Egli.
Natalia is out of surgery. All went as planned. Unfortunately, Egli cannot answer calls in the recovery room but will keep everyone posted and give you all updates as soon as Natalia is settled.
    Thank you for your continued love, prayers, and support during this time.

Pray on,
Aissa

February 20, 2009, 1:36 p.m.
Day 311 on our road to recovery

Dear Companions,

Thank you very much for your endless prayers, love and support which sustains us, allows us to feel God's presence through you. The past 24 plus hours have been intense for Natalia. As some of you already know, her surgery yesterday was a success, but she has been in excruciating pain since she got out of the operating room six hours later.

At around 5:50 a.m., her team of caregivers finally decided to change her pain medication and she is a bit more comfortable now. She was able to sit up on her chair for about 45 minutes this morning with a lot of assistance from occupational and physical therapy personnel.

This is a home stretch for her and I ask that you continue to pray for her strength. I don't have the words to tell you how courageous she has been and how strong she keeps pushing forward in the midst of adversity. She is indeed a warrior. She is my hero, and I am truly blessed to have this little angel teaching me to have faith and to embrace life with courage and strength in the midst of adversity.

In addition to having the upper part of her leg reconstructed yesterday, she had to have a bone marrow transplant from her hip to her leg. She also had a bone transplant to strengthen the upper part of the prosthesis. This sounds complicated, but I am repeating these words as I heard them. I trust the orthopedic surgeon and she felt that this is going to work on Natalia. We accepted the donation of a human bone which was crushed, mixed with her bone marrow and implanted into her leg. This is the explanation given to us and I am going with it. It is our only option. Amputation is not an option.

I want to see my daughter standing, walking, running again and I am willing to do whatever it takes to strengthen her leg, even having a cadaver's bone implanted.

Her knee replacement was left untouched. The new prosthesis was made five millimeters longer to allow her room for growth. There were no signs of infections or more cancer, thank God! This procedure has proven to be effective in the past on their patients. We are hoping and praying that it works on Natalia as well. We are trusting this can restore Natalia's leg and sooner than later, she can be up on her own two feet.

Today, her cheeks are rosy, and she looks beautiful and strong. She lost a lot of blood during the surgery and was given a transfusion again last night.

Again, thank you for your prayers. At times I can't even pray for myself and hope that God accepts my breath and existence as a prayer.

We continue to rise from the ashes like a phoenix. We continue to get up each day and keep pushing forward.

Keep on keeping on,
Egli - Proud mommy of a super warrior.

Egli Colón Stephens, Ed.D.

CHAPTER 14
REDEFINING OUR NEW NORMAL

Even there your hand will guide me, your right hand will hold me fast.
    - Psalm 139:10

Each of us will have to make the choices that allow us to be the largest versions of ourselves.
    - Julia Alvarez

February 24, 2009, 12:02 a.m.
Day 315 on our road to recovery

Dear Companions,

I write to you tonight from our hospital room feeling like a prisoner. I don't know where to begin, I am scared, overwhelmed, tired and I feel like I am suffocating. I turned on the computer to write over two hours ago, but I can't find the words. It is 2:03 a.m. and I keep staring at the screen as tears roll down my face. We are almost at our finish line and I am growing weary. We feel cramped in this tiny room that we are sharing with a newly diagnosed teen. As I look at the patient next to us, I listen to them and hold back from sharing too much. Everyone's journey is different and I don't want to impose our fears and share all the obstacles we encountered. I pray that she finds hope in knowing that she too can overcome this battle.

Natalia is making progress each day. I have been watching her sleep for the past few hours. She looks as peaceful as York Avenue looks from this ninth floor window on this cold night.

Our weekend was pretty quiet and our closest family members surrounded us. Natalia's hemoglobin kept dropping, and she received three other blood transfusions that seemed to perk her up a bit finally.

It has been amazing to witness how much faster Natalia is recovering now that her body is chemo free. She is blooming like a precious orchid. Each day she wakes up with renewed energy and she sets the bar higher.

Today, she walked for the first time since the surgery and did it gracefully. She took slow, firm baby steps down the hallway until she made it

to the finish line. The therapists assisted as she walked on crutches bearing no weight on the newly reconstructed leg,
Will.

I often wonder where she gets the courage from. She fights through the pain, obstacles and challenges day in and day out. I watch her breathe through them and push forward with determination. She walked around the corridors twice today and went upstairs to the recreation room. She asked me to put her on a wheelchair to shoot some pool.

Natalia worked hard and played even harder today. Although she had an upset stomach for most of the day, she pushed herself to get out of bed. She has had a fever for the past two nights, but we have been told not to worry about it because it is normal for the first 24-48 hours after surgery.

Each day she is less dependent on the pain medication and only presses her pump as needed. She remains connected to the drainage from the incision and a few IV bags but has been breathing on her own for the past few days. Although she hasn't been asking for her usual cravings, she has been eating solid foods on and off since Saturday night.

The bandages were removed this morning, and we were both surprised to see that the doctors reopened the entire previous 18-inch incision. We were unaware that they had to reopen the entire incision and not just part of it. We continue to be surprised. I don't want to question their medical procedures, but I am tired of surprises.

I thought I had asked all the right questions prior to the operation. This evening we met with her surgeon for clarification and she explained that to reconstruct the upper part of the prosthesis, perform the human bone and bone marrow transplants, she had to reopen the entire incision and unscrew everything. As complicated as this sounds, I am astounded at the wonders of medicine, our wonderful surgeon and God's greatness. My Humpty-Dumpty was put back together again and the future has never looked brighter.

Again, we would like to express our deepest gratitude to you for embarking on this journey with us, for your loyalty, for your love, healing prayers and support.

These hospital rooms and corridors are cold, sad and lonely, but I thank you all for your virtual loving embrace. Deep down, I am confident that all is well. We are restoring, recovering and recuperating.

All is in divine order. This too is coming to an end.

With hope and gratitude,
Egli

February 25, 2009, 11:43 p.m.
Day 316 on our road to recovery

Dear Companions,
   We are at home! Home sweet home!
   As this great nation rebuilds itself from the aftermath of 2008, we are also rebuilding our lives. It is time for restoration!

With our deepest gratitude,
Egli and Natalia

March 25, 2009, 10:28 a.m.
Day 343 on our road to recovery

Hello Everyone,

It is me, Natalia! I am happy to inform you that I have been recovering well from my second leg reconstruction and I am enjoying being done with chemo. I am also learning a lot from home instruction and yesterday, I reached another significant milestone in my recovery.

I had the Mediport removed. Mommy was scared, but I knew I was going to be fine. It was a minor chest surgery to remove the lines that transported medication and gave easier access to my bloodstream. I am home now, a little sore but I have been through worse.

Yesterday, I also had a few tests that confirmed that I continue to be cancer free. I declare myself cancer free for life. Thank You, God! I will praise Your name forever!

Please continue to pray for me as I begin physical therapy next week. My chest, arm and leg are hurting. I know this new challenge is going to be difficult, but I am going to keep my eyes fixed on the prize, walking again and hopefully, walking the runway.

XOXO,
Natalia

April 14, 2009, 12:37 p.m.
Day 365 on our road to recovery

Hello Everyone,

It is me, Natalia. I am writing from Weston, Vermont, a place that I love and where I have created many childhood memories skiing with mommy. Our friends, Honey and Michael lent us their country home for us to get away and restore ourselves. We brought my cousins, Kim and Dariela with us. I play with them a lot to give mommy a break.

Today is the first anniversary since my cancer diagnosis. It seems like another lifetime. I have been reflecting a lot about this challenging year.

"I have come a very long way."

I am happy to say that God's grace completely healed me. Each day I am feeling stronger and I know that my cancer days will soon be a distant memory.

Thank you very much for your prayers and support.

XOXO,
Natalia

May 8, 2009, 9:24 p.m.
Day 389 on our road to recovery

Hola,

It is Natalia again. Today was such a great day! I am so glad that I am healed.

I have not written since our Easter break in Vermont but let me just tell you that we had a blast! Thanks, Honey and Michael, for your generosity and for letting us stay in your vacation home. I had a lot of fun with my mom, Kim and Dariela. We were able to spend quality girly time with each other without the interruption of doctors, nurses and medication. Mommy and I needed this time away and it was so much fun!

We went to a farm nearby and fed a calf by the name of Katy. We fed her with a giant baby bottle, almost the size of a soda bottle. She drank it as if we were going to take it away from her. We also saw lots of cows being milked with machines.

We chased chickens on my crutches and petted the horses. We also went to my favorite country store in Weston and I played with toys I had not seen since my early childhood days. I bought lots of candies with my allowance and mommy did not bother me. These days she is not as strict with what I eat.

Mommy also dragged my cousins and me to see her Benedictine monk friends at the Weston Priory every day. Some days she wanted us to join her four times a day for their prayer services including morning prayers at 5:00 a.m. when it was still dark outside. Mommy would leave the house at 4:30 a.m. and drive her SUV through the mountains all by herself to be in God's house, but that did not work for me. My cousins and I prefer to meet God in bed. Mommy and I have a lot to be thankful for, but once a day with the monks was enough for my cousins and me. They are super kind and friendly, but I just want to play and feel like a kid again.

We also went into the town of Manchester, mommy's second favorite place in Vermont because of all the clothing stores and outlets. We were in fashion heaven and feeling like kids in Disney World. I visited my favorite designer's store, Betsey Johnson and bought myself a sweater with allowance from my dad that I saved up. I was excited! I wanted to buy everything. It was great to play dress up and try on different outfits.

Vermont is a very special place for me. Mommy has been taking me there since I was about three years old. We would go every year to ski camp at Bromley Mountain. It was really sad to see the mountains knowing I can never go skiing again. The doctors have advised me to avoid all kinds of activities that put me at risk of breaking my leg. I am grateful mommy exposed me to so much at such an early age.

Our lives are very busy with home instruction, physical therapy, mom's job search and my hospital checkups. We are redefining our lives again, but it is hard for mom and me to find the time to write updates often. Our days are busy, but we have lots of fun together.

We often take strolls at Central Park and eat our lunch by the garden.

She takes me to the playground where I enjoy spinning on a swinging tire. I am beginning to feel normal again. New York City is really beautiful in the spring and I am trying to catch up on all that I missed last year.

Today was an exciting day; my caterpillar kit arrived. In first grade, one of my favorite teachers, Ms. Cagnina, ordered butterflies for us to raise in the classroom and since then, I have been fascinated with butterflies. I went online, researched how to get the butterfly kit and bought it. I feel like a first grader all over again. I am so excited knowing that it will take a few weeks for the caterpillars to transform into butterflies. I plan to free them at Central Park.

I also had physical therapy today, and I am so excited to see that I can bend my knee to 90 degrees already. It has been a challenge to get to 90 degrees and hopefully by the middle of this month I will be walking with one crutch. I see my doctor on May 19th and I hope to walk without crutches by my 14th birthday in July.

Thanks for the continuous love, prayers, and support. God has been so good to us.

XOXO
Natalia

May 10, 2009, 12:02 p.m.
Day 391 on our road to recovery

Hello Everyone,

It is Natalia again. I want to wish everyone a Happy Mother's Day, especially to my mommy!

I am not with my mom at the moment. I am in Queens visiting my dad but I will see her later. I just want to thank you, mom, for everything you have done for me. You are the real deal! Thanks for sticking with me through thick and thin, especially through the thick.

Thanks for being by my side when I needed you the most, making sure I got the best care. Thank you for guiding me every step of the way. I just want you to know how much I love you. You are my rock, and the best God has ever given me. I love you with all of my heart, mommy.

Love,
Natalia

May 28, 2009, 1:53 p.m.
Day 449 on our road to recovery

Hello Everyone,

Thank you very much for keeping me in your thoughts and prayers. My checkup and exams went great last week. I continue to be and declare that I will forever be cancer free. Woohoo!

The only problem my orthopedic surgeon finds is that I am growing too fast. On the other hand, I enjoy being taller than my mommy. She seems to be shrinking as she is getting older, but the reality is I am outgrowing my internal prosthesis. The orthopedic surgeon briefly mentioned that the solution to fix this problem is to operate on my other leg, Grace, to stop the growth. Nothing further has been determined and we are not making any drastic decisions. We are all stunned by my rapid growth, but for now, no more surgeries. This summer is for healing, more healing and some fun as I turn fourteen years old.

On a happier note, I took my first step without crutches. It was really amazing to take my first step. I got nervous when my doctor opened her arms and told me to walk towards her. I took one step towards her and two steps toward my mom. Unfortunately, my mom did not come prepared with a camera for this awesome event, but I repeated it the next day and she took some pictures.

I continue to work hard in physical therapy. Sometimes I cry because of how difficult and painful it becomes, but in the end, I know all of my hard work will be worth it. I have some big plans for my life. Home instruction is going well. Next week I will take the state exams and I am already preparing for the end of the school year.

I am learning to accept life the way it is and counting my blessings. I am grateful for every breath and step I take.

XOXO,
Natalia

June 28, 2009, 10:16 p.m.
Day 480 on our road to recovery

Hello Family and Friends,

I am happy to announce that I am a Junior High School graduate now and this September, I will be a freshman in high school! Last week I was invited to attend the step-up ceremony at The Young Women's Leadership School, the school I attended before I was diagnosed and received an award from Mayor Bloomberg and the New York City Commission of Women's Issues. I was also asked to speak at my graduation. It was very emotional to return to school and see my friends as I delivered my speech. I was almost in tears!

I am sharing my speech here with all of you. I have to get things ready for a sleep-away camp that mommy is sending me to next week for children battling cancer and their siblings. I am already missing mommy. She really wants me to go, but I am not too happy about it.

As always, I will put my best foot forward and explore.

XOXO,
Natalia

Natalia's Speech delivered at
The Young Women's Leadership School- Eighth grade
Step-up Ceremony, June 24, 2009

Good Afternoon,

It is a great honor to be here today wearing The Young Women's Leadership School uniform. Thank you so much for inviting me to speak at this important step-up ceremony. The last time I wore this uniform was Monday, April 14, 2008. As many of you know, that was the day I was diagnosed with cancer. I was still in my school uniform when my mom took me to the doctor's appointment and we received the horrible news. That news turned our lives upside down. It has been a long and painful year and half, but I am back on top. I have won the battle and give God thanks for keeping me here and for giving me the strength to fight for my life.

I knew middle school was going to be challenging, but never imagined it was going to be this traumatic. It all started very excitingly when our assistant principal Colleen took all the seventh graders camping in Goshen, NJ. It was a big transition for most of us as we started seventh grade in 2007. I was struggling to keep up with all the hard work, homework and the many responsibilities that came with middle school.

As hard as it was to deal with seventh grade, I quickly realized it was nothing compared to fighting for my life. There were many days when I would see children of my age going to school in the morning while I was returning to the hospital to receive chemotherapy and continue lessons by my bedside. I missed school terribly and knew it was not as hard as what I was going through.

Today, I take with me great memories of the lessons learned and the wonderful people I have met here at TYWLS. Many who supported me and ran this marathon with me.

There are three things I know for sure and want to share

with you:

1) Life is a precious gift—treasure it.
2) Faith and fear don't go together.
3) You have to be grateful for everything in life.

LIFE: What have I learned about life? I have learned that the hardest thing about life is living with its ups and downs, but life overall is good. Love your life and live well because life as we know it can be taken from us at any time. What we thought would be a regular checkup for a pain in my leg, turned out to be cancer. In a minute, my life was on the line. As much as I wanted to hide in a hole for a few days, I decided to fight for my life instead and that, I did! Giving up was not an option in my mom's vocabulary. This experience has taught me to stop complaining about the little things in life and be courageous.

FAITH: Faith is what pulled me through this nightmare. Faith was my medicine. Faith works miracles. Faith is what made me a 13-year-old living miracle. Faith in God, faith in myself, faith in the world and faith in those who love me. I also learned that faith and fear could not exist together. Choose faith. When you choose to believe, you have to let go of fear and trust that everything will be fine.

GRATITUDE: I have always been grateful for everything, but I now have a new sense of gratitude. Gratitude is my new attitude. Being grateful in life is important. I am so grateful for every second of my life.

I am grateful for my doctors, nurses, teachers, friends, family and those who love me. I want to close by saying how grateful I am for every one of you here at TWYLS. It was not easy to finish seventh grade and complete all of the eighth grade in a hospital bed, but I am glad that I was able to graduate with all of you. I missed you all; your love and friendship helped me pull through this.

So go out and be a light to the world and live your life to the fullest!

Thank you.

August 13, 2009, 12:33 a.m.
Day 487 on our road to recovery

Dear Family and Friends,
Thank you very much for your love and support during this long and challenging battle. It is now time to let go of the past and embrace the new possibilities that the future brings.
This will be our last journal entry.
Natalia is doing great and is as precious as ever. Every time I hold her and look into those big green eyes, I feel a sense of peace because, in her presence, I experience God's holiness.
It has been a busy but exciting summer for us. Natalia turned fourteen last month and also graduated from middle school with honors. This fall, she starts high school in the Upper East Side. She is taking the bull by the horns and little miss independent is full of plans for the new school year.
I am having serious separation anxiety issues because Natalia chose to transfer schools. Although she loves everyone at TWYLS and knows they will treat her with the utmost respect, she wants a new beginning. She doesn't want to stand out, get special privileges, or be treated differently because of her condition. She prefers a clean slate and be in a place where nobody knows her. This is hard for me, but I am respecting and trusting her decision. After many pillow talks with God, my co-parent, my heart informs me to let her go.
God speaks to me with peace in my heart when I am making the right decision and anxiety when I am not. I am learning to listen to and follow my intuitions. This feels right, but I am struggling with transportation since she will no longer be across the street from my job and I will not be able

to drive her. She stands to my face often and tells me, "Mommy, I am 14." *"Ya mi que me importa"* I respond in Spanish. Being fourteen doesn't mean anything to me. I am having a hard time letting go.

It is difficult for me to forget the hardships we have been through, but all she sees is a bright horizon. I pray we can see eye to eye before I lose my mind as she continues to crave independence. I will be going back to work on the same day she starts school. I have arranged for a small yellow school bus to pick her up in the mornings and drop her off in the afternoon, but she is not having it. As a matter of fact, she is livid.

"You want to embarrass me like that, mommy? You are messing up my reputation. The kids at school are going to make fun of me. I am taking public transportation. You better cancel that service or I will not go downstairs."

This is what I hear day in and day out. I am at my wits end with this kid.

She went to a summer camp in Pennsylvania for a week and missed me like crazy. I found her sitting on her cabin's steps with the counselor ready to come back home, and yet, she wants me to let her go to school on public transportation. She was miserable the entire week she was away and only mingled with the counselors because of the hard time she had connecting with other kids her age. I had never seen my kid happier to see me. She greeted me with the warmest hug. She ran to me, screaming, "MAAAAAA!"
as if she had not seen me in decades.

This summer we resumed our annual, week-long, single parents retreat by the beach in Cape May. I was first introduced to this faith-based group by the Marianist Brothers when Natalia was eight years old. They have now become our new extended family and have been very supportive of us during this challenging journey. They have helped us redefine our family of two, heal the wounds of the divorce through their dynamic, children friendly ministry. We have had so much fun there throughout the years.

This is the only way we have been able to vacation on the shores every year. Natalia doesn't remember her dad and me under the same roof. As soon as I realized our relationship had come to an end, I left a month after her first birthday to avoid more trauma. Before our first retreat, we had never talked about the divorce.

We were sitting under a tree there when she asked me, "Am I divorced, mommy?"

I laughed uncontrollably and explained, "No, your daddy and I are divorced, sweetheart. Children do not get divorced. You have to be married before you get divorced."

"Oh, I get it now." She responded.

I did not say anything further. As a mom, I have learned not to over explain myself or give extra information. I often have to remind myself this, especially when asked difficult questions, as she often does. My motto is, keep it simple Egli, don't get diarrhea of your mouth.

These single parent's family retreats have been a lifesaver for us. They have helped us grow in our faith and cope with our everyday lives. I have been able to share my experiences in small groups and have also learned how other divorced, single and widowed parents are coping. We don't grow in isolation; we grow in community.

The summer adventures continue. Just two days ago, we got back from Hawaii since Natalia was granted a Make a Wish Foundation dream vacation. We went to Maui and Kauai for a week with Mami and Jenny. During this trip to Paradise Island, we realized it was time to put closure to this chapter of our lives and turn the page.

Our journey doesn't end here. Natalia still has a lot of work ahead in physical therapy to regain the flexibility and strength in her leg. We are staying focused on how much progress has been made and all that has been accomplished. We are keeping our eyes on the final prize, and our hearts fixed on Jesus. She no longer uses crutches to walk and the wheelchair has been returned. Hooray!

I am all set to go back to work at my former employer in September and we are finally adjusting to life in Manhattan. Even our little dog, Princess has adjusted.

God has been so good and faithful to us and we know that we are not alone.

Thanks again for all the support, encouragement, love and prayers. We are moving forward as always, *sin mirar atrás.* Thanks for fighting a good fight with us. We lost some soldiers in combat along the way, but they will forever live in our hearts. Thanks for standing strong and fighting until the end. We have won this battle!

With profound gratitude, peace and love,
Egli and Natalia, The Warrior

… Egli Colón Stephens, Ed.D.

PART 3

CHAPTER 15
PICKING UP THE BROKEN PIECES

So do not fear, for I am with you; do not be dismayed, for I am your God. I will strengthen you and help you; I will uphold you with my righteous right hand.
 - **Isaiah 41:10**

Father, I abandon myself into Your hands; do with me what you will. Whatever You may do, I thank you: I am ready for all, I accept all.
 - **Brother Charles De Foucauld**

"I am not taking that yellow bus to school mom; I have told you that you are going to ruin my reputation before I even start high school." Natalia grudgingly mumbles under her breath as she gets up from the dinner table and walks back to her room.

Figuring out how she will get to and from school has been our ongoing battle this summer. She refuses to take the school bus insisting that she wants to live a life as normal as possible now that she is done with treatments and is getting ready to enter ninth grade.

God, what should I do? I am scared! What if someone pushes her on public transportation? What if she slips when it rains or snows? I can't drive her to and from school, and I can't afford to send her in a cab every day. Doesn't the world know we just defeated Goliath? Don't they know we are just coming out of combat? How do I live again? How do I trust that the world is not going to defeat her now?

I have so many questions, so many fears, and so many doubts. It has been so hard to get to where we are today; I want to protect her from everything and everybody. This is such a difficult transition. I don't know how I'll be able to concentrate at work now that she won't be across the street from me.

Why did you give me such a defiant child? Why did she have to decide to transfer schools? Didn't you know I was going back to my old job? Why did she have to change the plans for me? Doesn't she know how complicated single parenting is? Would You please help me figure this out? It seems I come to You for everything, and I do because You never fail me. You are all I have. At times You are a very silent God, and although I don't see You, I know You are here. Each night, when I lay my head on this pillow, You comfort me as I pour my heart out and cry out to You. You are my refuge and strength. I know You hear me. I just know it. I know it, the same way the sun will rise in the morning.

I can't believe my sister is not backing me up on putting Natalia on the school bus situation. We disagreed a couple of times while in Hawaii when she approached me about letting Natalia take public transportation. Is she out of her mind? *Tía arcagüeta*, she spoils her rotten! What is wrong with them? I feel like they are both ganging up on me. Mami was our referee every time we argued, making our trip bittersweet. It should be forbidden to talk about serious matters when on vacation. The place was like paradise and not a place for arguments.

The separation anxiety is real, more so for me than for Natalia. She is ready to take over the world, but I insist on holding her back. I am having a hard time letting go and I feel like strapping a child harness on her as much as I hated the thought of it when she was a toddler.

Also, it still feels like a dream believing that we won the battle and are living victoriously. Each day my goal is to surrender and live like the winners we are. I can't allow the fear of cancer coming back to rob me of this moment's joy.

"I have an idea, mommy; I am going to show you that I can get to school on my own. Tomorrow, let us take the bus to school. You are going to walk a few steps behind me, far enough, but you know, I want you to see me. I want you to see me swiping my Metro card, transferring buses once I get across town to the East Side and then walking to my school on my own. I want you to see that I don't even limp, I even know how to climb the steps to get on the bus and no, I don't need a cane, walker or crutches anymore. I got this mommy. I know how to walk on my own again. After we get to school, I am going to show you that I also know my way to the hospital for physical therapy after classes. I can walk there; it is only a few blocks away. We will practice it a couple of times until you feel comfortable and then I am going to do it on my own, right?"

Sure, I replied, as I kept cleaning the stove and thinking, *Mira muchachita, you think you are all grown telling me what to do. You are only fourteen. Who do you think you are?*

"Ma, are you ready to go?!" Natalia shouts from her room. "Where are we going, Natalia?"

"Mom, I told you we were going to test run my trip to school. I am going to show you I can do this. Let us go. Get dressed."

She went into my closet and passed me some clothes. I thought she was kidding when she mentioned it yesterday. I had no idea she was ready to start her plan and of course, I had no other choice but to get dressed.

It was late August, and there was a cool breeze coming in from the window. The leaves were turning colors and beginning to fall, welcoming the new season. I grabbed my bag, my shades and we went out of the house.

"Before we get on the bus, let us go to the train station to get the Metro cards. Don't forget to walk a few steps behind me; just watch me." She signaled orders. She set off to the train station on 116th Street, just down the block from where we lived.

"Hold on to the rail Natalia to go down the steps," I shouted from a few steps behind. "Hold on tight."

Natalia wasted no time. She took off, making sure I maintained a distance. Now and then she would signal with her hand letting me know to stay further, but I could not help it and sat next to her on the bus. Again, she indicated with her index finger that I should sit in the back and watch her come off the bus to transfer. I sat in the back with my eyes fixed on her, attentively making sure she did not talk to strangers or stare. New Yorkers don't like to be looked at for too long. I could not help but think of all the horror stories my students shared in class about public transportation.

"Please keep your sidekick in your pocket; I told you not not to take your phone out," I said to her in a low tone from the back of the bus, hoping she could read my lips and understand my gestures. She rolled her eyes and put it away, signaling that we were getting off soon. I made my way out through the back door seconds after seeing her walk out the front door, feeling like a stalker.

The walk from East 79th Street to Eleanor Roosevelt High School on the Upper East Side was a long one. I kept thinking how exhausting this walk would be on her newly reconstructed leg.

"Why do you have to complicate things Natalia, when you can have a door to door service?"

I wish I had a personal driver every day.

I guess that in the mind of a teen, being dropped off in a school bus is a big thing. What do I know? That sure would not bother me!

"So we are here. I told you I had this down-packed mommy. I am not a baby anymore."

"I know," I replied firmly as I grabbed her hand and proceeded to walk.

I was under the impression that we were going to catch brunch in one of those outdoor cafés on First Avenue being that the weather was good and her mission had been accomplished, but she had other plans.

"No, mom, let me show you I know how to get back now. Let go of me and go back to your place. Watch me."

She grinned as if making fun of my attachment to her arm. I am sure she was hoping she had convinced me of her independence since it seemed like she was the mother and I, the obedient child.

We tried the test run one more time, but I never gave her a definitive answer on the traveling arrangements. I don't think she was expecting one either. She had made up her mind and was determined to go to school on her own, while I was still trying to figure out how I was going to force her to ride on the school bus. I refused to cancel the bus service.

"What are you wearing to school tomorrow?" I asked while she was in front of her bathroom mirror styling her little afro.

What once looked like peach fuzz was turning into a bushy, curly head of hair. I remembered how much I loved to adorn it with all kinds of barrettes and headbands when she was a toddler. Her cheeks are rosy and she now had a double chin from how well I have been feeding her. She wears a small or a size 2, women's size, and no longer the children's size 12 and 14 she was wearing when initially diagnosed. My little girl has blossomed into a beautiful young woman, and I refuse to acknowledge it, not to mention she is back to her monthly periods. Her doctor had to stop it abruptly upon her diagnosis. My poor girl had just reached puberty the week before we were informed of the horrible news.

"I am wearing my hot pink Converse, my favorite Levi's and a t-shirt. Do you think I am going to look cute, mommy?"

I followed her into her room and helped her pick a t-shirt. Still, there was no talk about how she is getting to school. We were both avoiding the subject. The last time I brought it up, she threatened that she was not going to school if she had to get on the yellow bus, but I am sticking to the idea that she will respect my decision, as she always has. I will walk her downstairs and she will obediently hop on the school bus as I wave goodbye, smiling.

***

"Good morning, my little sunshine. You are up early and ready to go. Come have some breakfast; it is ready."

We both sat down to have a toasted bagel with cream cheese and a cup of tea, but we were both too anxious to eat. Her backpack was all set with all of her supplies. I was concerned about the weight she would have to carry. Her school has been so accommodating with patients from Memorial Sloan Kettering. They agreed to order another set of books to keep at home, this way she doesn't have to travel back and forth with such a heavy backpack.

"It is time to go, mommy; I am leaving."

"Hold on. Let me take you to the bus; they will be here in five minutes."

"Mommy, please don't do this to me, I told you to cancel that service. I am taking a regular bus to school. I am fine; trust me. Go, tell them I am not going with them."

Her voice very firm as we both went out the door. The school bus was already in front of our building when we got to the lobby. I walked over to the bus driver and told him my daughter was not going with them. Natalia was determined and walked to the public bus stop as she blew kisses to me. I waved goodbye.

Into your hands, I commend her my sweet Lord. Please take care of my little girl and keep her from all harm and evil.

I was convinced she would change her mind after riding a crowded bus daily, but she never did. Every morning I would tell the bus driver that my daughter was not leaving with them. I felt so embarrassed. What a waste of resources, I thought as I sucked my teeth and held my head. Two weeks into the school year, I finally canceled the bus service.

***

I have learned to let go and accept my super resilient daughter. She now drives her own car and continues to take public transportation to get to places she can't drive to in New York City.

She has always refused to request a handicap permit, something her physician has suggested to make things easier for her. Each time I have reminded her about it, her response is always the same.

"I don't want to be labeled, mommy. I survived cancer. I can do anything. I don't need that permit."

I now know it was her unyielding spirit and God's grace that got her through the wrenching circumstances. We disagree at times, but there's nothing I want to change about my daughter. She is opinionated, strong-willed, decisive, consistent and very firm in her decisions.

I will never forget the day she grabbed my red stilettos and showed up to physical therapy with them as I pushed the wheelchair in.

"Not only are you going to teach me how to walk again, but you are helping me get into these heels. My dream is to walk down the runway." She told her physical therapist.

Natalia has accomplished amazing things. She graduated from high school with several prestigious awards celebrating her tenacity. One of them was in honor of a former teacher who had recently passed away from cancer.

She has participated in several school fashion shows and has been living her dream of modeling for designers, all while attending physical therapy.

During her junior and senior years, she assisted with the school's girls' basketball team since playing was something she was never able to do again. Her great love for the game has led her to stay involved. She also had to give up becoming a classical ballerina, another one of her dreams.

Her sophomore year was the most difficult. One of us was going out of the window and it was not going to be me. It took every ounce of patience to keep my sanity and not chastiste her with the *chancleta* because I noticed she was not performing to her full potential. It was then I decided on taking her to see a psychologist affiliated with Memorial Sloan Kettering, one that specifically worked with cancer survivors.

Her comments after the consultation were, "Your child is fine, Ms. Colón. She has adjusted well to her current situation and is not letting her past cancer experience affect her in any way, shape or form. Your daughter is perfectly fine. Perhaps, you might want to consider counseling for yourself; you seem to be very stressed." She recommended.

"Thank you. I do acknowledge that I am a bit stressed.

It has been a bumpy ride for lack of a better phrase. It has been difficult picking up where I left off and putting the pieces back together. Thank you. Is there anyone you can refer me to?"

"Here are a couple of numbers of highly respected colleagues. Feel free to set up an appointment with them."

"Thanks again, I will give them a call."

As I walked out of her office, I felt happy to hear that my kid was perfectly normal.

I need to let go of some of the tension and responsibilities that I feel are on my shoulders. But how do I let go now? How do I surrender to you, Lord?

That night, I went to bed feeling relieved knowing that my daughter was not traumatized by her experience, but was worried about what was causing her grades to drop. I noticed a disconnect in her. Suddenly, she had lost her ability to manage time and was not thinking about the consequences of her actions. She also began lying to me.

"Natalia, did you do your homework?"

"Yes, mommy; all of my work is done. I am ready for tomorrow."

It was as if she was assuming her responsibilities were going to go away if she ignored them. I was so aggravated by the situation that I wanted to smack some sense into her. At the Parents-Teachers-Conferences, I would hear something different than what my child was telling me at home.

"Natalia is missing homework. She did not submit her term paper. She seems distracted and does not participate in class."

These were the comments I would hear from her teachers. As an educator, I felt like a failure. Hearing praises from parents on the effect I had on their children made me feel worse. *How could I not have that same effect on my child? Why can't I get her to keep up with her work?*

I was devastated and took her teachers comments very personal. I was angry at her for not seeing the impact this could have on her future and I was determined to fix it. I took away all privileges which were not many, and had her on lockdown.

At the next doctor's appointment, I brought this issue to her medical team's attention, and they referred her to NYU for a neuropsychological evaluation to see how her brain was functioning.

"Don't worry, mom; she may be experiencing chemo fog." Her doctor said.

"What is that?" I asked.

"It is mental cloudiness caused after cancer treatment." She responded.

I left there feeling worse than when I left the Parents-Teachers-Conference. I felt guilty for the pressure I had been putting on my daughter and how harsh I was on her.

God, please help me. I hope my daughter's brain is not fried. I can't handle another problem. I don't recognize the way she is acting at times. Is this what it is like to be a teen? She has been too sick to rebel on me and now it is coming all at once.

I fell asleep while having this conversation with God. I was drained.

As soon as I got my first break at work that morning, I called the neuropsychologist's office to schedule an appointment. A series of tests were done which resulted in no damage to the brain. *Thank You, Jesus!* I left there feeling relieved and ready to take matters into my own hands.

***

The ride home was a quiet one. We took the M1 bus all the way home. I was suffocating with anguish and could not bear being submerged underground in the subway, so we chose the bus. The entire time, Natalia looked out the window in despair. I am sure she worried about what my next step would be. She knew I worked a tight shift and did not play around when it came to school.

I felt so much relief to hear there was no brain damage caused by the treatments.

Thank You, God! Thank You for hearing my plea and for seeing my desperation. Thank You, but how do I discipline a child that has been critically ill? I don't know how to do this. I need to keep the bar high and continue to set high standards. The world is not going to make any excuses for her. How do I do this? I don't want to pity her.

We were both drained when we got home and went to sleep after dinner.

The next day, I woke up refreshed, invigorated and ready to figure this out. I am going to whip you back into shape; I thought to myself when I said goodbye. *Yo te voy a meter en cintura muchachita,* you don't play around with me. I saw fear in her eyes; she did not know what to expect from me.

On my way to work, it occurred to me that I was going to try what we do with our at-risk students with Natalia when they need some adjustment - I *am going to put her on academic probation.* I drafted a contract of expected outcomes between her teachers, her and me. I was merciless. I contacted all of her teachers, including her principal. I wanted all of us to be on the same page. I scheduled her to attend tutoring with them before and after school. I accounted for every minute of every hour of each day until she could show the ability to manage her time and improve her school performance. I also hired a home tutor to help her prepare for her Social Studies Regents examination.

I placed a digital clock by her bedside with AM/FM radio and an alarm. There was no television during the week and weekend privileges depended on the feedback I received from all of her teachers through a weekly group email. They would sign her log in sheet daily with her time of arrival and any additional comments. I instructed her to drop off her log-in sheet along with her cell phone in a basket I placed by the entrance on our kitchen counter. Her routine for the time being, was to shower immediately upon getting home, have a snack, take out her clothes for the next day, do her homework, feed the dog, eat dinner and go to bed. These were all the rules I had written down for her next to the corresponding time on her daily schedule. I tucked her in every night and prayed with her after kissing her goodnight. The only thing allowed during bedtime was reading or writing in her journal – no electronics were used in the bedroom.

As exhausting as this was, I had to be consistent with this method of discipline to teach her structure again. I kept this routine until the end of the school year and because of it, her grades and attitude improved tremendously.

I realized then, that I had to continue being the stern and loving parent I had always been. After setting the bar high, she rose to the occasion.

***

Junior and senior years were a breeze. She was also given the opportunity to visit Paris and Barcelona with the Foreign Language Program. Quite frankly, she exceeded my expectations, and I was thrilled.

I had been so consumed in raising my daughter, overcoming the obstacles and furthering my career that it did not occur to me to ask God for a lifelong partner, a husband. I remember a time when Natalia said to me, "Mom, I am going to college in four years. What are you going to do with yourself? You better start dating!"

I was shocked to hear this from my little girl. I never

expected her to be concerned about my dating life. She followed her comment by telling me that I looked too good to stay single for the rest of my life and that it was time to stop hiding behind my books and find a boyfriend.

"Mom, you have more degrees than a thermometer! Get out and start dating!"

Dating was not something I was interested in doing, at least not until she was off to college. I was very conscious about who I brought around her, especially if I saw no future with that person.

I wanted to teach my daughter by example and bringing men in and out of her life was not going to happen. Our home was our sanctuary, and I wanted to keep it that way.

However, that night, I went into my room with a smile on my face, *Hmmm, that is not a bad idea after all.* The thought of having a companion to share my life with sounded amazing!

I realized that my soul was craving for this possibility. I longed for the warmth of a partner like never before, and throughout the weeks to come, there was a tremendous shift in my soul. For the first time in a very long time, I felt I could make myself emotionally available. My prayer soon changed, and I began asking God for a husband.

One night, I got on my knees and asked, Lord, *bring someone into my life that loves You so much, that in loving You, he will know how to love me.*

A couple of months later, love found me again and I met Lance, my answered prayer. He is the most honorable, kind and gentle man I know. He loves me like no other because he loves the Lord with all his being. We dated for five years and then I married the man of my dreams shortly after Natalia's nineteenth birthday.

It was an unforgettable day! My parents walked me halfway down the aisle and then Natalia met me with my bouquet and gave me away at the altar. We had a beautiful garden ceremony followed by a grand celebration. He is perfect for us, and we have made a great family.

***

College-life has been quite an adjustment for Natalia. She decided to stay in New York and has managed to balance her modeling career, her studies and working with children with special needs. Although she is undecided about her major, she knows she wants to work with children.

These days I feel more at peace.

For a long time, I held my breath after her regular and continuous medical follow-ups. There came a time when I finally decided to stop worrying and learned to live by faith and not by sight. My child has been cured and I will rejoice in that victory. I refuse to live in fear, especially when Natalia does not. I declare life and blessings over my daughter's life.

***

Natalia has fulfilled her dream of modeling. On two separate occasions, she modeled for renowned designers during New York Fashion Week. On February 18th, 2015, she made her dream a reality when she was selected to model at the Mercedes Benz New York Fashion Week at Lincoln Center. Admission was restricted, but after so many years preparing in physical therapy, I was determined to see my daughter walk down the runway even after several unsuccessful attempts. Since she is no longer a minor, she doesn't need a companion. Thankfully, God made a way. I was able to go in with a group of parents accompanying their small children who were also modeling. I accompanied a child whose parent could not attend and I was able to see my daughter fulfill her dream. After seeing Natalia walk the runway, there's no doubt in my mind that my daughter was born to model.

It was effortless for her. She was in her zone! I was a proud mother taking pictures of every chance I had.

Children come with their dreams, and they show us how they need to be parented if we allow them to. The ar-

Mercedes-Benz Fashion Week for Stello by Stephanie Costello and Michael Costello (Left.)
New York Mercedes-Benz Fashion Week 2016 - Walter Collection by Walter Mendez (Right.)

ticle I published on NBC News Latino on May 19th, 2015 continues to attest to this.

***

Last fall, Natalia had major leg reconstructive surgery again to correct her internal prosthesis. Since the initial diagnosis, we have known that the prosthesis is not permanent.

There still isn't one that lasts a lifetime. Less than two years after her last reconstruction, she broke her kneecap when she fell from the top of the stairs at her best friend's sleepover in January of 2010 and had been in pain on and off since then. She was out of school for a couple of weeks after that incident with a brace and crutches. She seemed to have healed, but throughout the years, the pain and inflammation escalated because of the wear and tear that was done to the leg.

Last year during her annual checkup, her new orthopedic surgeon told us he could correct the problem. I could not believe my daughter had been living with pain for almost eight years! The thought of being in an operating room again and the recovery process kept us from exploring other possibilities.

At first, we were hesitant about another operation. Natalia, being older said she now knew what to expect, but the possibility of a pain-free life sounded better. We needed some more time to process the information, get other opinions and build the strength to go back into combat.

The problem was trusting our new surgeon; we had established a relationship with our former orthopedic surgeon who had done an outstanding job. We were willing to travel to John's Hopkins Hospital in Maryland, where she is now the Chief of Orthopedic Oncology, but our health insurance did not approve the travel outside of our city for the procedure.

Thankfully, the six-hour surgery was a success! Natalia's new orthopedic surgeon did a fantastic job and we could not be more pleased. He collaborated with a plastic surgeon who closed up the incision since the same scar had been opened a few times before. As customary, I remained silent and in prayer at the hospital chapel.

We remained one with each other and with God.

A week later, my girl was already walking and determined to walk the runway for Fashion Week. Her post-operation work in physical therapy paid off and once again, she walked the runway.

Natalia modeling during New York Fashion Week in February 2016, months after her inner prosthetic leg revision on her knee - opening her 15 in. incision and learning how to walk again.

Natalia has been speaking her dreams into existence since childhood, and as a mother, I feel fulfilled. My co-parenting with God has worked out terrifically. I remain humbled and in awe of His magnificence, protection, and provision.

***

As her 21st birthday approaches this summer, she is preparing to embark on a different journey. She has been granted admission to a school on the West Coast and will continue to pursue her modeling career there as well. This will be bittersweet for me as I am already missing her, I don't know how to live without her. *No se vivir sin ti chiquita.*

She reminded me that God's blessings reach everywhere and that God will be with her all the way in Los Angeles.

Vé con Dios mi niña querida, follow your dreams and never forget all you have overcome. May God's blessings be with you.

Natalia's first photoshoot at 12 years old directed by her aunt and stylist, Jennifer Colón in Brooklyn, NY. It was always her life-long dream to become a professional model, however, her dreams were put on hold as months later she was diagnosed with Osteosarcoma.

CHAPTER 16
FAITH AND FEAR DO NOT COEXIST
EPIGRAPH BY NATALIA HARRIS

For I know the plans I have for you, declares the Lord, plans to prosper you and not to harm you, plans to give you hope and a future.
      - Jeremiah 29:11

It is up to you to squeeze the juice out of life every day, wake up with a grateful heart no matter what is blocking your road and fulfill your lifelong dreams. Be a burst of sunshine.
      - Natalia Harris

Like the cherry blossoms that bloom in New York City in April - ten years later and today, at age twenty-two, I continue to bloom and evolve. My cancer days are long gone, and my memory of those years are foggy. I am glad my mother kept this journal and we can use it to look back at our journey; a tribute to the life God has granted me and a reminder of His love, mercy and favor.

"Natalia, my precious gift from above, my Earth angel, you were just a baby when you chose to live by faith and not by sight. In your darkest hours, you held on to hope and taught me how to do the same." My mother says.

She recalls one day while I was at the hospital receiving chemotherapy that I woke up and told her, "Stop worrying so much about my health mommy. You are a woman of faith, and you have to choose which side you are going to be on because faith and fear don't go together."

When she told me the story years later, it was a blur to me. "Some wise and prophetic words for a twelve-year-old," I said.

Through it all, I knew in my heart I would be healed, but I never imagined that the blessings God has bestowed upon me would be this big. Coming from a family deeply rooted in the Christian faith, I know of no other way to live. I have chosen to hold on tight to God's promises for my life, my dreams and to never give in to my fears.

***

"Natalia, fear is false expectations appearing to be real." These words which were whispered in my ears by my ski instructor long before my diagnosis will forever stay with me. I was at the top of Bromley Mountain in Vermont, staring at fear in the face and repeated this to myself over and over again until I was able to let go. I have held on to this mantra throughout my life and don't know where I would be had I given into those false expectations appearing to be real - FEAR.

As I write this last chapter on the tenth anniversary of my cancer diagnosis, I must admit this journey has been terrifying. It has been difficult and uncertain amongst other things, but my faith and the faith of those whose shoulders I stand on, is bigger than any fear that comes my way. Though my love for fashion and modeling took a back seat while I fought for my life, today, my life has evolved, and I have come full circle. Ten years later and after a grueling process, I have emerged. I find peace in knowing that life is not linear and despite mine taking some significant shifts and turns, I am reminded of the Footprints poem by an unknown author:

"The Lord replied, my precious, precious child, I love you, and I would never leave you. During your times of trial and suffering, when you see only one set of footprints, it was then that I carried you."

Therefore, each morning, I wake up grateful for another day, knowing that those who love me pray for me daily. I take it one day at a time. I take deep breaths and speak to the fears that try to prevent me from living my best life.

"Go away. I don't walk alone; come another day," I say.

***

It was the spring of 2016 during a trip to Los Angeles when I decided to embark on a new journey and move to L.A. to attend college and seek new modeling opportunities. I was enveloped by the warm sun-kissed air, beautiful hills, palm trees and the beach breeze LA offered. This was the perfect opportunity to be on my own, something I had been itching to do. So, I enrolled in Santa Monica College and chose to move into a beautiful studio apartment in West Hollywood.

Though this decision crushed my family's heart, my decision felt right. I was grateful to have my dad's support from the very beginning, but sadly, my mom was torn. Nonetheless, she held my hands and through her devastation, furnished my apartment, decorated my space and helped me unpack as we both discovered my new city. It was a place where I could be on my own and not have to give up my dreams of becoming a model.

While in LA, I completed my Associate's degree then, continued freelancing and networking in the fashion industry: working with top designers in Los Angeles Fashion Week. As my mom's only child and having the challenges I have endured, I have lived a very sheltered life. Nevertheless, Los Angeles gave me the going away experience I was yearning in a non-traditional way. I discovered parts of myself I did not know existed and learned to love myself more intimately. I made great friends, explored the new city, cherished love and to be loved and most importantly, became closer to God. My time in LA was brief and after a year, I realized I could not be away from my family. T hough my decision to move back to New York seemed impulsive, I knew it was time to go back home, to the place that nurtured my dreams. I am currently finishing my Bachelor's Degree and looking into graduate school.

Trusting my internal GPS and listening to the whispers of the Holy Spirit continue to validate that coming back home was the right decision. After ten years of attending many casting calls, networking, knocking on doors at different modeling agencies, I have accomplished a lifelong dream.

It was the coldest day in January and the worst snow storm we had during the winter of 2018, "The Bomb Cyclone." I refused to cancel the casting I had been waiting for my entire life. I stood there in disbelief and in less than five minutes my mom and aunt unbundled me from all of the winter gear, slipped on my stiletto boots, loosened my curls from the silk scarf under my hat and handed me my portfolio. As I entered the elevator, I prayed and on that fateful day, my dream became a reality. I was signed to STATE Management Modeling Agency and I am working for all the brands I have always dreamed of!

Could this really be happening? Am I really here?

With each passing floor, I breathed my fears away. I was greeted outside the elevator by one of the agents.

"You take the award for the bravest model!"

They were stunned. I was one of the few models who did not cancel despite the bad weather conditions, but I was determined to take what was mine. I have learned to show up no matter what regardless of the storms that come my way. Accomplishing this lifelong dream of mine was a surreal moment and I could not help but wonder if the storm outside was symbolic of the storms I have overcome in my life. Being filled with vision and purpose, my faith and connection with God have deepened.

***

Having everything in my life fall into place and in divine order, reaching a milestone also means returning to Memorial Sloan Kettering Cancer Center for my annual checkups. This year is extra special; my tenth anniversary of being cancer-free, the day I was born again. As my annual appointments approach, I speak positive affirmations and envision God's healing hands over my leg. During my showers, I ask God to wash away any impurities and bless every part of me. Entrusting my life through this visualization and a power higher than myself has been my saving grace and all my fears are washed away. Yet, entering Memorial Sloan Kettering (MSKCC) is nerve-wracking knowing the fears and nightmare of what others are living. Instantly I become nostalgic and relive those moments of nausea, the picks, probes and the inevitable anxiety of the possibility of cancer coming back or the thought of the chemo having affected an organ as I have been warned. However, as challenging as it is for me to walk back into that building, I always pray that my presence can be of some comfort and give hope to those suffering. Not only was this anniversary surreal for my family and me, but also for the doctors, nurses, and staff who have witnessed this miracle unfold through me. Knowing how far I have come and watching me grow into the accomplished young woman I am today is a testament. The experience, to say the least, is bittersweet.

I made it!

I say these words with conviction. These words carry a different meaning for me, one that cannot be bought.

I made it because i won the cancer battle.

I made it because i got up after every chemotherapy and every feeling of defeat when i thought i could not take another day.

I made it when i knew the patients next to me did not survive and i heard the agonizing cries of the families that surrounded me.

I made it when i walked out of that hospital never to return for treatment.

I made it when i went back to school and no longer had to be homeschooled or pitied by those that knew my story.

I made it when i graduated high school and santa monica college.

I made it when one by one, my dreams have become realities.

I made it because i am here today, having not taken a single moment for granted and living my purpose of hope, love and faith. I am grateful for my family and forever indebted to the entire team at Memorial Sloan Kettering Cancer Center for the extraordinary care they provided and for fighting this battle with me.

While cancer is something I do not wish on anyone, this experience has taught me valuable life lessons which I will carry with me forever. Fighting for my life has made me resilient, persistent, grateful and mindful, but I must admit there are times when I feel as though I am trapped in the body of eighty-year-old. On those days when I experience excruciating pain and aches, I feel a disconnection between what my mind wants to do and what my body is capable of doing. There are many times when I have had to give up certain activities I simply could not do because of my internal prosthesis, but I quickly remind myself: Natalia, nothing is more precious than the blessing of living life cancer-free. I have learned to surrender and allow myself to walk in the path God has predestined for me, always appreciating this second life opportunity.

My life is a tribute to faith and answered prayers from my family and people all over the world. Cancer did not have the final verdict - my dreams, my zest for life and everything God created within me, did. Thanks to everyone that has surrounded me, I am blessed and highly favored beyond measure. We are all wounded warriors and survivors in one form or another and I am a living testimony that my fight against cancer, my surgeries and my post-treatment journey can give hope and comfort. I write these lines with tears of joy, freedom, purpose and most of all, gratitude.

I understand and accept the responsibility God has given me and I will live the rest of my days sharing my journey and becoming all that He intended me to be and remind others that miracles do happen. Amazing grace, I once was shattered, but now, I remain **UNBROKEN.**

GLIMPSE OF NATALIA'S MODELING PORTFOLIO

GLIMPSE OF NATALIA'S MODELING PORTFOLIO

GLIMPSE OF NATALIA'S MODELING PORTFOLIO

Natalia Harris

May 2018
Central Park
Photographer: Jacqueline Ayala

For I know the plans I have for you, declares the Lord, plans to prosper you and not to harm you, plans to give you hope and a future.
       - Jeremiah 29:11

ACKNOWLEDGMENTS

My most sincere gratitude is to God, my Creator. Thank You for Your constant presence in my life. Thank You for getting us out of the wilderness and bringing us to the Promised Land. Thank You for being my co-parent and a light of guidance in my times of darkness. Thank You for healing my daughter and placing her feet on solid ground. For as long as I breathe, I will live to give You honor and glory, and I hope this book is a testimony of our unwavering faith in You. Thank You for placing the vision of this book into my heart before I knew how it was going to unfold.

To my parents José and Obdulia "Lula" Colón for the gift of life, unconditional love and for sacrificing your dreams to make sure ours were fulfilled.

To my brother and first friend Claudio Colón, and my loving sisters Annié and Jennifer Colón, for the bond we share. You are all my earth angels. Our love for each other and art runs deep – we are all artists in our own way.

To my niece Kimberly Penelope and nephews, Kevin, Duke and Lennox... Oh the places you will go my little ones! Remember that you come from a line of overcomers on whose shoulders you stand on. Being your Titi is one of my greatest joys.

To my mom's late sisters, Mercedes "Mecho" and Rafaela "Faela" for showering me with their maternal love and for teaching me all that I know about being a mother. *Mami gracias por traerme al mundo y compartirme con tus hermanas, su amor materno ha llenado mi vida y hoy soy la madre que soy por la manera que ustedes me han amado.*

To my grandparents, for instilling their faith and devotion into my DNA.

To my friends, #squad. Thanks for becoming family and for your unconditional love and support.

To my Vermont sisters and their families. Thank you, prayer warriors! You knew my place was by my daughter's side and you did everything in your power to make sure of it. Natalia and I are eternally grateful to you and love you beyond words.

To my Cristo Rey New York High School community, The Young Women's Leadership School, The Church For All People, Holy Innocents R.C. Church, Dimensions in Dance, Weston Priory, Cape May Marianists. Thank you! You all exemplified the true meaning of faith in action and a community at work.

To Natalia's Nana. Thanks for your compassionate and tender heart. You are a phenomenal woman and an amazing grandmother to our Natalia.

To Natalia's care team at Memorial Sloan Kettering Cancer Center. Thank you for putting my Humpty Dumpty together again.

To my untiring editors and dear friends, Carmen Inguanzo and José Albino for their keen eye, attention to details, generosity, and sensitivity with this project. It took us almost two years of frequent meetings in my kitchen while I cooked for them and endless late night conference calls to get this manuscript to what it is today. After I thought I was done, Carmen took the manuscript for another round of editing and revisions where she taught me the descriptive art of showing the reader on the page instead of telling them. She also showed me that less is more and I painfully learned to let go and shave the story. Thank you both for your valuable time and energy while you still managed all of your responsibilities. I treasure your talent and friendship.

To my dear friend Yesi Morillo for wiping off my tears and believing in me at a time I thought this manuscript would never turn into a book. Thanks for your guidance and edits. This was a monumental project and you treated it with the utmost respect and kindness.

To Oyindamola Shoola - Once my student, now my friend. She has come into my life to make sure this book makes it to your hands. Thanks for being my final reader, editor, and reviewer. Thank you for writing such an insightful foreword to this book. Your encouragement, diligence and guidance throughout this process are greatly appreciated. The world awaits your greatness. You are such a gift to me and to this world!

To our cover designer Morenike Olusanya, our photographer Jacqueline Ayala, the make-up artist for the cover photoshoot, Shaina Eve Cintron, and Jennifer Colón's overall creative direction. Thank you! You are indeed a dream team.

To Alexandra Z. Charney, the missing piece to our publishing dream team! Alex, you came at the 11th hour to make Unbroken greater than what it already was. Thanks for all the hard work that went unseen behind the scenes, your patience, compassion and sensitivity to this project. No mountain was too high for you to climb and obstacle to overcome. It has been a pleasure to bring you into our journey. We treasure your expertise and value your friendship dearly.

To my beloved and supportive husband Lance, thank you. You have redefined what marriage means to me. I love being your wife. *Te amo.* You are the epitome of excellence and my happy ending.

To all those fighting against this merciless disease, especially to my godmother Milagros "Lalo" Estrella. *No pierda la esperanza. Pa'lante.*

To all the readers, thank you for embarking on this journey with us. Believe and remember that the human spirit is unbreakable when grounded in faith.

Despite the many obstacles both mother and daughter have encountered, they both find great satisfaction in giving of themselves to others. They both served as missionaries in 2012 by joining Mercy Medical Mission and a team from John's Hopkins Hospital, where they contributed as Spanish medical translators in Perú. Over the past decade, they have participated and assisted in leading family retreats at the Marianist Family Retreat Center in Cape May.

EGLI COLÓN STEPHENS, Ed.D. is a woman of deep faith committed to social justice and transformative education. She has been an inner-city educator for about twenty years and currently teaches Sociology at Bronx Community College and Dominican History at Borough of Manhattan Community College, in New York. She is a firm believer that education transcends all barriers and has the power to empower, and liberate people.

Dr. Colón Stephens is a New York State Certified teacher. She obtained a Doctorate Degree in Urban Education from the Graduate Theological Foundation. As part of her doctoral studies, she completed a fellowship at the University of Oxford, the United Kingdom, in Interfaith, Inter-religious dialogue and the history of Christianity. Her academic prowess, intellectual acuity and social acumen at the Graduate Theological Foundation and Oxford University led to her getting a unanimous nomination by the faculty to receive the highest academic award in Hispanic Studies named the San Juan Diego Prize, based on the strength of her doctoral thesis, "Urban Education in a Holistic Environment."

She holds a Master's degree in Urban and Multicultural Education from the College of Mount St. Vincent where she graduated Summa Cum Laude with a cumulative 4.0 GPA and a Bachelor's degree in Healthcare Management from St. Francis College. She is also a Certified Holistic Life Coach, a consultant and a professional lifestyle model represented by STATE management.

Dr. Colón Stephens has been a distinguished human

rights guest speaker at many institutions, including the United Nations, Fordham University, Universidad Panamericana de Aguas Calientes in Mexico to name a few. She is passionate about Latino literature and writing. Her writings have been published on NBC News Latino, My LifeStyle Magazine, Mamás Latinas and a brief article-critique on the Oprah Magazine. She has also been featured in Super Canal 33, The Observer, La Jornada, The New York Times, Fitness Magazine, SemiPerm Connections and Life Coach Network Radio.

Her road to excellence began very early in life. She believes that her accomplishments have everything to do with discipline, love for learning, tenacity and a sense of cultural identity. In spite of her humble beginnings in Santiago, Dominican Republic, she is highly accomplished and proudly admits that her greatest accomplishment has been raising her daughter while pursuing her educational and professional goals.

For more information and updates, please visit:
eglicolonstephens.com
Photographer: Jacqueline Ayala

NATALIA HARRIS is a professional model signed to STATE Management, cancer survivor and body positive image activist. She was born and raised in New York, and her family is from the Dominican Republic and Barbados. Ms. Harris earned an Associate Degree in Liberal Arts from Santa Monica College and is currently completing a Bachelor's degree in Journalism. She has had major health setbacks which have all led to a pivotal moment for a significant comeback.

Ms. Harris has participated in New York Fashion Week at Lincoln Center for designers of the stars such as Michael Costello, Walter Mendez, Candice Cuoco, Vanessa Simmons and Council of Fashion Designers of America (CFDA) Vogue finalist Rebecca de Ravenel, to name a few. She has been featured in Women's Health Magazine, Cosmopolitan Magazine, The Morning Show in Australia, Telemundo's Un Nuevo Día, Refinery 29. She stars in David Guetta and Black Coffee's music video, Drive. She also filmed a commercial for the Borgata Hotel & Casino airing on several mainstream channels. Ms. Harris is also featured on a few episodes of Project Runway season 17 on Bravo TV, and has been featured in a campaign for fashion brand Six 02 by Foot Locker displayed across a Times Square billboard. She is one of the faces for an ad by Delta Airlines and has modeled for global makeup brand Laura Mercier.

Natalia Harris is determined and crystal clear about spreading a message of hope to the world. Although she loves fashion and modeling, her life's purpose is to use it as a platform to heal humanity. She hopes to empower other young women and little girls to embrace life with its perfections and imperfections, to keep a positive outlook in life and to never give up on their dreams. The trials and tribulations she has courageously faced have made her the resilient young woman that she is today. She is a resilient woman of faith and strength that aspires to inspire in everything she does.

For more information and updates, please visit:
iamnataliaharris.com
Photographer: Kate Moore

UNBROKEN

Social Media and Contact Information:

Follow Unbroken via Instagram:
@UnbrokenTheJourney
and #unbrokenthejourney

Follow Unbroken via Facebook:
UNBROKEN THE JOURNEY

For all inquiries and feedback, please send an email to: unbrokenthejourney@gmail.com